*wholehearted and unequivocal praise for*

## From Woe to WOW: How Resilient Women Succeed at Work

*"You're stronger than you think!"*

"It wasn't until I read *From Woe to WOW* that I realized how valuable a resiliency book written just for women could be. Patricia Morgan is the perfect author to write this book. In it she draws on her personal life experiences, knowledge of human resiliency and expertise as a coach, trainer and facilitator. The result is a resiliency program that covers emotional processes, inner complexities, and relationship dynamics with more sensitivity, understanding and depth than is found in resiliency books that men prefer to read. *From Woe to WOW* is a valuable resource for women facing a wide range of rough experiences."

AL SIEBERT, PhD, Director of The Resiliency Center
and author of *The Survivor Personality* and *The Resiliency Advantage*

∽

"*From Woe to WOW* is a wonderful, practical, inspirational tool for women and all those who support them!"

DR. ROBERTA NEAULT, award-winning specialist in career/life management and author
of *Career Strategies for a Lifetime of Success* and *That Elusive Work-Life Balance*

∽

"When you combine real-life stories with heaping portions of practical how-to tips, relevant ideas and inspiration, you end up with a recipe for real life success. No empty calories here—this book is the real deal!"

MICHAEL KERR, speaker and author of *Putting Humor to Work*

∽

"*From Woe to WOW* is filled with stories and practical strategies for managing some of the most difficult situations women (and men) face in work and life. Patricia embodies the amazing resilience of the *WOW-Empowered women* she features in her book. Read it not only for hope when you're on the brink of despair, but for the practical tips and tools you need to live as the *WOW-woman* you really are."

NELL SMITH, Certified Career Development Professional
and author of *Change and Transition: The Path from A to B is Not Always a Straight Line*

"This book is not your typical self-help book. It is a book to be treasured as your bible because it honors you. It is a book filled with wisdom and strategies to accept your imperfections while empowering you to celebrate your strengths. Patricia has given us the biggest gift of all—permission to celebrate with abandon, to live life without guilt and to know that we are stronger than we think. Patricia gives you the know-how to turn your Woes into WOWs."

ROZ USHEROFF, International Specialist in Corporate Communication, Business Protocol and Executive Presence and author of *Customize Your Career* and *Taking The Leap: Leadership Strategies in Turbulent Times*

~

"*From Woe to WOW* is chock full of information, suggestions, guidelines and case studies that will empower you to control your own life and career. This book will inspire, challenge and guide both women and men who want practical tools to create their desired lives."

CAROLE KANCHIER, PhD, educator and author of *Dare to Change Your Job and Your Life*

~

"Patricia Morgan brings a lifetime of experience and wisdom to answer the many questions women have about how to truly 'handle it all' with grace, ease and a feeling of accomplishment and satisfaction; she lives it every day and is a role model for women world-wide. Yes, this is the book that will allow you to be truly inspired to design the life you deserve…WOW!"

VALERIE CADE, CSP, Past National President CAPS, Former CEO and author of *Bully Free At Work*

~

"From start to finish, Patricia Morgan's *From Woe to WOW: How Resilient Women Succeed at Work* is a jewel. Sharp, finely-honed and brilliantly illuminating, Morgan helps women see their own reflections more clearly by showing them other ways to imagine the largest and smallest choices in their lives. Every page of this book offers wisdom, wit and practical advice. WOW is right!"

REGINA BARRECA, PhD, author of *It's Not That I'm Bitter: How I Learned to Stop Worrying about Visible Pantylines and Conquer the World*

"In *From Woe to WOW*, Patricia Morgan aptly describes resilience-in-action, blending poignant stories of real women in real life situations with valuable tips, insightful exercises and strong advice. It's a worthy read!"

JANIS FOORD KIRK,
author of *Survivability: Career Strategies for the New World of Work*

~

"Treat yourself to a high-energy book full of nurturing guidance, designed to build resiliency for the busy woman. Full of stories from real women's lives and practical tips that both build understanding and point out new possibilities, *From Woe to WOW* offers the advice that women deserve to have. Fast paced, readable and utterly delightful. This is one book that can change your life."

PATRICIA O'GORMAN, PhD,
author of *Dancing Backwards in High Heels: How Women Master the Art of Resilience*

~

"A wonderful book, full of great tools and meaningful insights to increase self-esteem, confidence and resilience!"

ANN COOMBS
author of *The Living Workplace* and *Mini Reflections*

~

"We tend to take resiliency for granted until life throws us a personal or professional punch—an illness, divorce, an overbearing boss or an uncooperative co-worker. Women are expected to bounce back quickly and quietly. But how? Stretched between work responsibilities and family obligations, there is simply no room for recovery. *Woe to WOW* gives us the tools to bounce back from any adversity. It is a must-have for every woman's tool box or giant, over-stuffed purse!"

FRAN HEWITT
author of *The Power of Focus for Women*

~

"I love Patricia Morgan's book! It just flows! Extremely practical and touches the heart at the same time. I will definitely be encouraging many of my clients to order it."

SUSAN MACCULLOCH, Psychologist

Published by Light Hearted Concepts

1411 – 25A Street SW
Calgary, Alberta, CANADA  T3C 1J8
Internet: www.solutionsforresilience.com
e-mail: patricia@solutionsforresilience.com
Phone: 403 • 242 • 7796

**Library and Archives Canada Cataloguing in Publication**

Morgan, Patricia, 1946 –
    From woe to wow : how resilient women succeed at work / Patricia Morgan

Includes bibliographic references.
ISBN: 978 – 0 – 9813046 – 0 – 1

    1. Self-realization in women.  2. Resilience (Personality trait).
3. Self-actualization (Psychology) in women.  4. Success—Psychological aspects.  I. Title.

HQ1206.M656 2009              158.1082              C2009 – 904135 – 9

CREDITS:
Cover, interior design and production: JEREMY DROUGHT, *Last Impression Publishing Service*, Calgary, Alberta <**lastimpression@shaw.ca**>
Cover image: OLIVER CHILDS, Ladybug and daisy, 2008. ©istockphoto / File # 6670248
Interior line drawings: ANGELIQUE GILLESPIE, Calgary, Alberta <**amariart@shaw.ca**>
Editing: ELISSA OMAN, Calgary, Alberta
Proofreading: SHARON HORSTEAD, Calgary, Alberta
Printed and bound in Canada by *Houghton Boston*, Saskatoon, Saskatchewan

**Disclaimer:** This book is not intended to replace professional, medical or psychological help.

*"You're stronger than you think!"*

# From Woe to
# WOW

Patricia Morgan

*"You're stronger than you think!"*

# From Woe to
# WOW

## How **Resilient** Women
## Succeed at Work

Light Hearted Concepts
Calgary, Alberta, CANADA

## WOW-Empowered Woman

She was crying and complaining, "Woe is me."
Traumatized—not knowing whether to fight, take flight, or freeze.
But then she realized she was stronger than she knew.
With resilience to face what was definitely untrue,
she soaked in the tub and called her friend,
and moved from Woe to WOW in the end.

PATRICIA MORGAN

# Acknowledgements

APPRECIATION is extended to all the amazing *WOW-Empowered* women I interviewed and who generously gave of their time and wisdom; the women in my audience who shared their experiences of adversity; and my friendship circle, who encouraged me and continue to do so.

Editor, Elissa Oman, stayed patient with my creative ideas and mistakes to help make this a well-structured and valuable resource. Proofreader, Sharon Horstead, provided an attentive eye to spelling and grammatical detail. Dr. Al Siebert, Nell Smith and Dr. Roberta Neault provided experienced and wise guidance. Award winning artist, Angelique Gillespie, added her feminine and visual touch.

My husband, Les, with his experience as a corporate ombuds—the gender-neutral term for ombudsman—offered knowledgeable counsel. Jeremy Drought, as ever, designed a book that is appealing to the eye and easy to navigate.

# Contents

Acknowledgments ......................................................... ix

Foreword ....................................................................... xv

Introduction .................................................................. 1
    Like a Carrot, Egg or Coffee Bean ............................. 1

## I · About Resilience · 5

What's Any of This Got To Do with You? ........................ 7

Beginnings of Resilience ................................................ 8

Rubber Band Principle .................................................. 9

## II · Evaluate Your Resilience · 11

Internal Resilience ...................................................... 12

External Support ......................................................... 15
    Resilience-Building Families and Homes ................... 15
    Resilience-Building Workplaces ................................ 16

## III · Demonstrations of Resilience at Work · 19

The Resilience-Generating Questions ............................................. 20
Name Your Woes ......................................................................... 20
WOW-Empowered Women .......................................................... 21
Woe to WOW Map ...................................................................... 22
    Internal Woes ...................................................................... 23
    External Woes ...................................................................... 23

WOW-Empowered Stories – Internal Woes ................................. 24
    1. Self-Doubt ........................................................................ 24
    2. Despair ............................................................................. 26
    3. Guilt ................................................................................. 28
    4. Workaholism ................................................................... 31
    5. Perfectionism .................................................................. 33
    6. Physical Limitations ........................................................ 35
    7. Learning Differences (Disability) ..................................... 38
    8. Focus on Weaknesses ....................................................... 41
    9. Lack of Education and Experience .................................... 43
    10. Self-Silencing ................................................................ 46

WOW-Empowered Stories – External Woes ................................. 50
    1. Criticism .......................................................................... 50
    2. Blame ............................................................................... 53
    3. Verbal Abuse/Bullying ..................................................... 55
    4. Sexual Harassment/Assault .............................................. 60
    5. Sexism ............................................................................. 62
    6. Intolerance ...................................................................... 67
    7. Moral Dilemma ............................................................... 69
    8. Business Betrayal ............................................................. 72
    9. Spousal Betrayal .............................................................. 75
    10. Caregiver Demands ........................................................ 78

## IV · Strengthening Your Resilience · 83

Reservoir of WOW Strategies ........................................................ 84

### I · Protect Your Inner WOW Woman · 86

1. Establish Clear Boundaries ............................................... 87
2. Align with Integrity ........................................................ 91
3. Keep Your *Humanness* .................................................. 93
4. Embrace Your *Womanness* ............................................. 95
5. First, Care for the Mother ................................................ 97
6. Choose *Your* Best Life Rhythm ....................................... 98
7. Get Familiar with Protective Laws .................................. 102

### II · Nurture Your WOWness · 104

1. Put Pollyanna to Shame: Think Optimistically ................ 105
2. Sweet-Talk to Yourself ................................................... 109
3. Honor Your Feelings ...................................................... 112
4. Move Out of Painful Feelings ......................................... 115
5. Have a *Good* Cry ......................................................... 117
6. Lighten Up! ................................................................... 120
7. Attend to Your Body ...................................................... 122

### III · Communicate with WOW Power · 125

1. Be a Dear with Two Ears: Listen .................................... 126
2. Speak Up: Assert or You'll Blurt ..................................... 129
3. Breathe and Get Grounded ............................................. 134
4. Ease Conflict ................................................................ 137
5. Plan for Resolution ........................................................ 139
6. Filter Criticism: Offer Feedback ..................................... 142
7. Manage Management ..................................................... 145

### IV · Take WOW Action: You Can Do It! · 149

1. Champion Change ........................................................... 150
2. Acknowledge and Demonstrate Your Strengths ............................. 151
3. *Make Up Your Mind*, Decide ............................................ 154
4. Demonstrate Courage .................................................... 156
5. Go Back to School, *Maybe* ............................................. 158
6. Be Laid Off without Laying Down ....................................... 160
7. Quit or Resign ........................................................ 161

### V · Connect for Added WOW Power · 164

1. Give and Receive Acknowledgement ...................................... 165
2. Be a Brazen Gal: Self Promote ......................................... 167
3. Get a Little Help from Your Friends ................................... 169
4. Nurture a Supportive Love Relationship ................................ 172
5. Create Your Village ................................................... 174
6. Give up Your Grudge ................................................... 176
7. Seek an Inclusive and Respectful Workplace ............................ 179

Conclusion ............................................................... 181
Endnotes ................................................................. 183
Resources ................................................................ 197

# Foreword

*by Dr. Roberta Neault*

*F*rom *Woe to WOW* is a wonderful, practical, inspirational tool for women and all those who support them! Right from the Introduction through to the comprehensive list of resources at the end, *From Woe to WOW* kept me fully engaged—I read it from cover to cover on a cross-country flight. With stories of real women sprinkled throughout, supported by a seamless integration of factual research and insights from the author's own rich life experiences, this book provides tips and strategies for turning life's biggest challenges into opportunities to shine. Patricia doesn't sugar coat the stories—in some she definitely shares the ugly side of life but without wallowing in misery. Readers will be inspired by the creative ways that women bounced back from traumatic experiences and will learn how significant others such as employers, friends and family members can become more supportive during challenging times.

*From Woe to WOW* is organized into four parts. Part I is a backgrounder on the topic of resilience. Part II focuses on evaluating resilience using a simple assessment tool that provides readers with immediate feedback; case examples also help readers to reflect on their external supports. Part III provides comprehensive lists of internal and external woes and then provides rich "WOW-Empowered stories" to illustrate how real women turned tragic situations around; each story is summarized with bullet-pointed life lessons: *Herstory Take-Aways*. Particularly appealing were *The Rest of Herstory* sections—it was comforting to know that life had continued to be positive and that the "Woe to WOW" experiences were more than transitory events. Part IV provides a *Reservoir of WOW Strategies* followed by five topical sections each with seven strategies for "WOW-Empowerment."

I'll be recommending this book to my colleagues, counseling students and clients, as well as my daughters and sisters-in-law. Patricia has done an amazing job of sharing stories of challenge to inspire women to be the best they can be. Women of all ages, cultures and backgrounds will find stories that resonate—this is a must-have resource.

Dr. Roberta Neault is an award-winning specialist in career/life management, a counsellor-educator, keynote speaker and author of *Career Strategies for a Lifetime of Success* and *That Elusive Work-Life Balance*.

*Port Coquitlam*
*British Columbia*
*May 2009*

# Introduction

*F*rom *Woe to WOW* is based on the strategies that real women use to recover from difficulties experienced at work and home. You will read inspiring stories and practical ideas for strengthening your bounce-ability. You will be better able to pick yourself up, dust yourself off and get back on your path whether it be at work, at home or in your community.

Why a book focused on women? Although women of this generation have many advantages over their mothers and grandmothers—more education, more money, more decision-making power and more career options—many of us still struggle to feel powerful, competent and resilient. Women still tend to accept responsibility for the majority of tasks for home and family no matter the number of their paid work hours. Women also tend to be socialized to focus on relationships and want them to be in harmony. Women don't feel as comfortable with competing as their male coworkers and peers. These factors necessitate that their resilient strategies somewhat differ from the majority of men. In the 1970s when women flooded the workplace they tended to minimize their feminine strengths and wore pin-striped suits. Now women have the opportunity to increase the ability of workplaces to encourage resilience for all employees through humane and empowering strategies. This book will help men and women come to a greater understanding of the challenges that both face in the workplace.

Eleanor Roosevelt said, "A woman is like a tea bag. You never know how strong she is until she gets into hot water." I invite you to join me and the women in this book in becoming stronger. I invite you to become your own *WOW-Empowered* woman.

## Like a Carrot, Egg or Coffee Bean

A young woman—distraught, discouraged and disappointed—went to her mother for advice. Without saying a word, her mom led her into the kitchen and proceeded to boil a carrot, an egg and a handful of coffee beans. Puzzled, her daughter asked her what she was doing. How was this going to provide her with an answer to her dilemma? The mom quietly instructed the daughter to observe the condition of each ingredient.

The daughter noted that the cooked carrot was soft and mushy and the egg hard. The coffee beans, however, had not changed at all. They were still the same shape and the same texture.

The mother pointed out that the ingredients are like people. At some point in our lives we will be thrown into hot water. We will face adversity. Who we are and how we respond will determine the end result. Note that:

- The carrot was initially strong but, after being in the hot water for a few minutes, its fiber weakened.
- The raw egg was fragile but fluid. The first egg that the mom placed in the hot water cracked—its insides spilling out of its cracked shell. The mom tried another egg. This time, the egg developed a hard outer shell. It was equally hard inside. There was a gray ring around the yolk and the egg white was tough and rubbery.
- It was only the coffee beans that remained impervious to the adverse conditions. The coffee beans changed the water to an intense dark brown color and filled the room with a rich aroma.

The mom then asked her daughter, "When faced with adversity, how will you choose to respond?"

*At some point in our lives, we are all asked the same question.*

*From Woe to WOW* includes a compendium of stories of women who have faced adversity. Some of their initial responses weakened their will and hardened their hearts. Yet all of them learned to effectively strengthen their resilience, bounce back and move on. They became *WOW-Empowered* women.

If you tend to walk into situations feeling strong and determined yet somewhere along the way your integrity is compromised and your soul destroyed, this book will assist you in taking baby recovery steps. If you once had a soft heart but, through trials and tribulations, became hardened on the inside and rigid on the outside, this book will help you once again find *joie de vivre*. Regardless of past choices or present circumstances, this book will give you the tools to change your beliefs, your habits and your future.

*Patricia Morgan*
*Calgary, Alberta*
*May 2009*

# I

# About Resilience

*Learning,*
*"You're stronger than you think!"*

As Chief Nursing Officer of Cornwall Community Hospital, HEATHER KLEIN-SWORMINK was accustomed to dealing with stress. Working with more than 400 nurses in an acute-care hospital was challenging but it was a job she loved. Heather had a gift for identifying foreseeable problems and encouraging her staff to be the best they could be. Under her leadership, the hospital earned a reputation for providing quality care. Patients and staff held her in high esteem. Her personal life was happy and balanced as well. With a supportive husband, she was able to attend to the demands of work and the challenges of raising four young children.

One day her situation changed. A surgeon with a questionable background joined the hospital staff. When Heather voiced her concerns, the hospital CEO responded with, "No, we want him. He's a friend of..."

Almost immediately, Heather began receiving negative reports regarding the new surgeon. Post-operative complication rates were high. Operating room, intensive care and emergency room nurses complained about the surgeon's poor decisions and unprofessional behavior. The pharmacy expressed alarm over the inappropriate drugs being prescribed. Patients filed reports of sexual advances. For eighteen months, Heather was a constant filter between patients, staff and management.

Your life may have followed a similar path. Everything that you have worked so hard for is coming together and then something happens turning everything upside down: an illness, a death, a divorce or an unscrupulous co-worker. This was certainly true for Heather.

Rather than being supported, Heather was verbally attacked. One physician accused Heather of making up statistics. Another physician came into Heather's office and said, "Stop with this! You better stop or you'll be gone!" In spite of the attacks, Heather continued to document the escalating occurrences of alarming incidents. Then there was a questionable patient death. The CEO refused to file Heather's reports with the hospital board. The tension escalated to the point where, in a meeting, the CEO raised his hand as if to hit her.

Heather was no longer merely concerned. She was terrified. Heather realized she was being told to violate medical and professional codes of ethics and to remain silent. The accusations, threats and pressure began to take its toll. Heather started to question herself. Months of being treated like a witch hunter left her emotionally and physically drained. The CEO used budget restraints as an excuse to lay her off. It took all Heather's energy to prevent this crazy situation from consuming her life.

~

Like Heather, I've also questioned and doubted myself. Although I've worked with colleagues and managers who behaved critically, abusively and sometimes unethically, my longest-lasting challenge has been as mother to our adopted daughter, Kelly.

It was during my first career as an Early Childhood Educator that my husband and I and our three-year-old son, Ben, welcomed six-year-old Kelly into our family. She came to us bright, articulate and physically adept in spite of experiencing a failed adoption and a number of foster homes. It wasn't long, however, before difficulties began to surface.

Regardless of all my training, behavior management skills and child development knowledge, I didn't cope well with the negative reports, school expulsions and Kelly's erratic behavior. Back then we had neither an Attention Hyperactive Deficit Disorder (ADHD) nor a Fetal Alcohol Syndrome (FAS) diagnosis and were left without appropriate support and treatment.

By the time Kelly was thirteen, she was skipping school, running away from home and using recreational drugs. Also by this time, I was an Early Childhood College Instructor and Parent Educator providing solutions for others. My professional identity took a battering and my behavior at home became erratic. I detached with calm or lost my temper, withdrew or sought support, pleaded or screamed, sought answers or crumbled into a weeping heap. The distress on my body necessitated visits to the hospital for irritable bowel syndrome attacks, a cardiac arrhythmia attack and an overnight in the psychiatric ward.

## What's Any of This Got To do with You?

Perhaps you haven't had to deal with a frightening work situation or a severely troubled family member but you have had mornings when it was hard to get out from under the covers. Maybe you haven't faced some of the misfortune, trauma and abuse that headline our newspapers. Yet most of us find some aspect of our lives difficult. Indeed, the American Institute of Stress reports:

> More than a third of workers (35 percent) say their jobs are detrimental to their physical or emotional health and 42 percent say job pressures are interfering with their personal relationships; half say they have a more demanding workload this year than last.

You might be in a situation like Heather was where your career, your reputation and any future job prospects are suddenly eroded. Or you might be in a place where your relationships are in turmoil. Your family and friends may believe that *all is well* at your house, at your place of work and in your heart. But you may find yourself saying, "This is just too hard."

As you read the stories in this book you may also be thinking, "They had it really rough but I am not sure their situations apply to me." The fact is they do apply to you. We all deal with challenges. Our workday may include delays, downsizing, staff shortages, reorganizing and office politics. Our home life can include burned lasagna for dinner, a broken washing machine, a long phone call from a lonely mother-in-law, a toddler's temper tantrum or a teen's hormonal outburst. You might think that your life isn't all that bad—that you don't need coping strategies—you just need more holidays, a shorter work day, a more supportive spouse or fewer household chores. Yet, if you are like most women, feeling overwhelmed has become your *normal* and you no longer notice the distress. Until, that is, you are faced with a wake-up call: a serious illness, a disgruntled partner who walks out the door or the loss of employment. Although there are no quick fixes, there are strategies that can help you weather the storms. And you need not stay stuck. There is a quality that sustains and helps us bounce back from adversity. Researchers call it *resilience*.

## Beginnings of Resilience

Most of us think that if we didn't have adversity, we would be happy. But we have it all wrong. Life is meant to be rewarding, happy, meaningful and challenging. Well-being with authentic happiness is the reward for conquering challenges. We open ourselves up to a meaningful life when we overcome adversity. But a meaningful life isn't just handed to us all at once. It comes as we develop resilience. Resilience refers to people's ability to cope with, adapt to and rise above hardship and crisis. It also refers to a cluster of *protective factors* or *interdependent capacities* which function like a reservoir of stress-hardiness resources. Resilience is strengthened as we nurture and develop a sense of ourselves, when we become impassioned by what we want and when we realize what strengths we have.

Focused research on resilience began in 1955 by Dr. Emmy Werner who spearheaded a 30-year longitudinal study with nearly 700 infants on the Hawaiian island of Kauai. Her study identified a number of protective factors for typical youth vulnerabilities such as physical and mental illness, addictions and delinquency. The result was a list of resilient-contributing factors. By the 1970s, *resilience* was a common psychological term. Researchers have continued to look for the protective factors that help people sustain a positive perspective and the strategies they use to recover from setbacks. They look for people who have satisfactory outcomes regardless of their unfavorable environments, function competently under significant pressure and recover effectively from trauma or crisis. Here are some assumptions about resilience from Stephen James Joyce's best-selling book, *Teaching an Anthill to Fetch*:

- Resiliency is the ability to adapt, bounce back and recover in harsh or challenging conditions.
- Resiliency is an innate capacity that we all have.
- Traits of resilience have been identified and we are able to strengthen them further with specific exercises.

## Rubber Band Principle

The concept of resilience is complex yet simple. It's as simple as the metaphor of a rubber band. Rubber bands, like people, come in different sizes and are subjected to different challenges. If you stretch a rubber band to its maximum, it usually springs back. That's because rubber bands are primarily made from natural rubber. Natural rubber has a superior elasticity. It is made up of minute threads that, when stretched, untwist and unbend—sort of like becoming unglued. If you stretch these threads too far, the rubber splits. The rubber band then snaps, cracks and breaks.

The metaphor of the rubber band is also complex. The modern rubber band goes through a process called *vulcanization*. This gives the rubber durability with increased elongation and the flexibility to snap back. Manufacturers routinely check the rubber bands for break strength and how much stretch the bands should be able to endure. Under normal use, a band will not break. Expose the rubber band to adverse outside influences such as heat, however, and the rubber quickly deteriorates. Keeping rubber bands cool helps maintain their flexibility.

A rubber band is weakened and often useless after being exposed to heat. People also function best when we are not stretched beyond normal use and when we are able to *keep cool* under adverse situations.

Fortunately, we are not rubber bands. We can bounce back stronger after our own personal and professional *walks through fire*. When we use basic hardiness and wellness strategies, we become resilient. The result is increased confidence, flexibility, health and vitality. For organizational bottom liners, this means improved results not only in adaptability to business change but improved employee productivity, problem solving, collaboration, retention and work satisfaction.

~

Even though Heather's capabilities were challenged and her ability to endure difficult circumstances was stretched beyond breaking point, she did not break. She had family and colleagues who supported her. She had confidence in her own capability. She refused to apologize for speaking out against injustice. On reflection, she said:

> I knew that in the long run, someone would replace me. I would move to another city or transfer to a different hospital. But my patients would not have the same opportunity. They still needed an advocate. They still needed care. The nurses I worked with also needed someone to stand by them. Some people might say that I was too self-sacrificing. But I believe we are all charged with standing up for what is right. In my position, I had a duty to protect my patients from incompetence and arrogance. I didn't want to ever have to look back and wonder if I could have done more.

Heather's beliefs, self-talk, confidence and support strengthened her resilience and helped her overcome a difficult situation.

I was not so fortunate. My work was so dramatically affected by Kelly's unpredictable behaviors and my subsequent collapses that for years I only accepted part-time employment. Trying to have a normal home life was just about impossible. When Kelly ran away from home for the final time, life actually became easier but was still filled with daily worry and the occasional disturbing phone call. As she battled a cocaine addiction, Kelly spent the next eleven years in and out of jail.

Your story will not mirror exactly my story or even Heather's story. But there will be similarities. You have, or someone close to you has, been tested, gone through incredible challenges, had to overcome unbelievable obstacles and walked through fire. You might still be walking through fire but all the better reason to read and put into action the tools offered in the following pages.

# II

# Evaluate Your Resilience

RESILIENCE is the ability to bounce back and effectively adapt to challenges and hardships. It also refers to the hardiness to successfully face adversity.

Not one of us is resilient all the time to all the same challenges. You may find *doing marriage* easy while your friend slugs through serial relationships. You may struggle with small workplace mistakes while your colleagues breeze through them. The literature on resilience speaks of the human ability to toughen up, to accept situations as they are, to explore choices and to take action while primarily maintaining a positive expectation. These resilience basics can be learned and strengthened.

Some say, "Resilience is one percent heredity and 99 percent persistence." You can persistently use resilience-strengthening strategies to help you retrieve the best of yourself, many of which are described in this book. Celebrate the strategies you have in place and take action to improve the rest.

## Internal Resilience:
### — Where personal coping strategies are developed...

Your internal world of beliefs and self-talk are shaped from the time you were pulled or pushed from your mother's birth canal. You learned ways to succeed from significant caregivers and role models. How emotionally, mentally and physically healthy those key players were affected you. Even if your caregivers and role models weren't healthy, you still have a choice, as an adult, to strengthen your resilience.

People who are more stress hardy have a strong *internal locus of control*. They assume responsibility for their actions and decisions. As Mary Kay, the queen of cosmetics and pink Cadillacs, said, "One of the secrets of success is to refuse to let temporary setbacks defeat us." Resilient people seldom view themselves as helpless victims. In messy situations, they quickly assess their options. Resilience and positive psychology studies provide guidance to assess our reservoir of hardiness-strengthening habits and attitudes. Take the following quiz to assess your resilience.

*Learn what you've got inside when calamity comes your way.*

## Assess Your Resilience

Rate yourself from Never to Always in the following areas:
Never (0) Seldom (1) Sometimes (2) Frequently (3) Always (4)

**Attend to Your Body:**

1. ☐ I recognize when my body is feeling distress.
2. ☐ I deliberately relax my body when I realize it is in distress.
3. ☐ I eat a wholesome diet.
4. ☐ I get adequate rest.
5. ☐ I routinely exercise.

**Attend to Your Feelings and Thoughts:**

6. ☐ I take charge of my thoughts in stressful situations.
7. ☐ I minimize my critical self-talk and increase my supportive self-talk.
8. ☐ I accept my feelings as is and use them as a personal gauge.
9. ☐ I know and use my strengths—at work, play and service.
10. ☐ I accept life's contradictions and ambiguities.

**Attend to Your Communication:**

11. ☐ I change negative comments into positive phrasing.
12. ☐ I listen to others and communicate clearly my position.
13. ☐ I work towards finding a mutual agreement in conflicts.
14. ☐ I minimize my criticism of others while offering helpful feedback.
15. ☐ I assert myself by saying *yes, no* or *I will think it over*.

**Attend to Your Social Support:**

16. ☐ I feel close and connected to significant others.
17. ☐ I give and receive help, support and listening time at home and work.
18. ☐ I express appreciation to others at home and work.
19. ☐ I encourage and act as a team cheerleader at home and work.
20. ☐ I make amends when I cause harm or inconvenience and am able to forgive others when they harm or inconvenience me.

**Attend to Giving Your Life Meaning:**

21. ☐ I learn and give meaning to mistakes, hurts and disappointments.
22. ☐ I view work, relationships and life with realistic optimism.
23. ☐ I set and meet realistic goals and expectations.
24. ☐ I laugh at myself while taking my responsibilities seriously.
25. ☐ I find purpose, optimism, pleasure, gratitude and meaning in my life.

_____ TOTAL / 100

## Scoring the Test

Please note that, even when our score seems to indicate otherwise, there may be times when we feel we can no longer cope with life's challenges. If that is the case, please call your local distress center immediately.

- **Bounce Back Champ** (Score above 75+):
You have developed a strong resilience factor. You use a combination of self-care strategies such as supporting yourself with affirming self-talk, choosing a healthy life style, creating a supportive network, developing an optimistic attitude and accepting responsibility for your pain, laughter and purpose. The stories and strategies in this book will give you ideas on how to strengthen any weak areas as well as tips on how to be a champion for others.

- **Bouncy Challenger** (Score between 50 and 74):
You have developed a moderate resilience factor. While you have strength in some areas of resilience, other components need attention. Celebrate what is working and take an inventory of the weaker aspects of your resilience IQ. Note the questions on which you scored low. The stories and strategies in this book will help you develop a plan that will support you as you work on all aspects of your resiliency.

- **Bouncing with Struggle** (Score between 35 and 49):
While your life has been seriously challenged with setbacks, you have retained enough resilience and strength to keep going in the face of adversity. You are encouraged to set a plan in place. As you read this book, note the stories and strategies that most resonate with your life. Then make note of specific ways you can improve your ability to remain stable and bounce back from the challenges that threaten your well being.

- **Bouncing Low** (Score below 34):
Please check in with your doctor. You may be at risk for depression, migraines, irritable bowel syndrome, heart disease and myriad other illnesses. By working on your physical, mental and emotional well being, you will relieve your loved ones of much worry and be able to create the life you deserve. This will be your first step towards rebuilding your confidence. Please use this book to support you in strengthening your resilience.

**Note**: Although this quiz is based on resilience research, neither it nor the scores have been formally validated. It is intended to provide basic information to serve you so you have the tools to move from Woe to WOW. The quiz is also available at <www.solutionsforresilience.com>.

## External Support:

— Where resilience is strengthened by healthy connection…

## Resilience-Building Families and Homes

*Hang out where they treat you right:*
*Live where you feel the love at night.*

Years ago, I counseled a young woman who had been yet again laid off from her job and was presenting herself poorly at subsequent job interviews. The reasons soon became apparent. Rachel's family circle was extremely toxic. Her husband called her a "stupid broad!" As a child, her domineering father told her to, "Shut your mouth!" Of course, Rachel struggled to believe in her own worth and abilities. A few hours of counseling were no match for the messages she received as a child or the messages she was receiving as an adult. As far as I know, she never left the toxic home environment that was slowly destroying her soul.

Compare Rachel to my fearless feminist friend, Laura Wershler. Laura grew up being supported, included in intellectual discussions and encouraged to speak out against what she perceived to be injustices. Bringing up children to voice their opinions and believe in themselves results in adults who can then take action based on their beliefs.

Laura had this to say about her upbringing:

Some of us, like me, take our supportive families for granted. I feel sad when I hear or read about lovely, intelligent women who doubt themselves because of harsh messages received as children. One of my most resilient characteristics is the ability to brush aside rejection, criticism and mean-spiritedness against me as more about the other than about me. Some would call this egotism or conceit but I wouldn't agree. I am also self-aware enough to learn from each experience how to adjust my behavior and communication to get along with just about everyone while always remaining true to myself.

As an adult, Laura is well prepared to take actions based on her convictions. She lobbied for effective sexual health education in schools, served as the board president for Planned Parenthood Federation of Canada, became the Executive Director of Sexual Health Access Alberta and is a frequent media commentator on sexual and reproductive health issues. Her advocacy for women's autonomy in sexual and reproductive health has resulted in condemnation and her fair share of criticism. Yet her passion to speak out for the rights of women never wanes. Laura was fortunate to have a forward-thinking mother and encouraging father. Laura's husband, Cleve, is one of her most sustaining supporters. He acknowledges her intelligence, knowledge and life purpose. The people closest to Laura encourage the best in her and the whole world benefits.

Laura's advocacy for women has spilled over into other areas. She became aware of the Dove Campaign for Real Beauty which celebrates women regardless of their shape, size or age. Laura entered her picture and profile in a Canadian campaign and was one of eight women chosen from over 7,000 applicants to be featured in Dove's August 2007 magazine, *Shine*.

Laura's authentic silver-gray hair and her confident self-esteem were deemed to be in alignment with Dove's empowering message that every woman deserves to feel beautiful and believe in herself. As Laura said, "I followed the campaign from the beginning and really appreciated the philosophy, which is about real women and real beauty."

## Resilience-Building Workplaces

*When you go to work it should be safe to show your brains and heart.*

Laura also surrounds herself with staff, board members and friends who are in alignment with her passion, beliefs and actions. Connections at work can help strengthen resilience. We have all heard the term toxic workplaces but how do they look, sound and feel? Ann Combs, author of *The Living Workplace*, wrote, "My definition of a toxic workplace is one without honest human relationships. It has nothing to do with the physical environment or sick-building syndrome. It has everything to do with lack of truth in committing to what is important for the wholeness and well-being of employees." She goes on to describe the key signs of a demoralizing or resilient-weakening work environment—employee lethargy, absenteeism, verbal and physical intimidation, sexist or racist comments and foul language. Our work environment affects our emotional, mental and physical health and consequently our productivity, focus and job satisfaction.

In a conversation with Nan Henderson, international speaker and expert in resilience, she mentioned that all environments—families, schools, communities and work places—either strengthen or weaken resilience. She said that *Fortune Magazine*'s

"100 Best Companies to Work For" are all organizations that provide workplace environments where strengthening resilience can be seen in action.

Here is what researchers describe as conditions that nurture resilience:

- Open, clear and consistent communication
- Opportunities for meaningful participation
- High expectations for success
- Opportunities to connect with others
- Leadership that provides healthy role models
- Available guidance and help
- Freedom to express feelings and concerns
- Opportunities to have fun
- Reasonable freedom to learn from mistakes
- Consistent expectations and boundaries
- Acknowledgement and support of strengths
- Recognition of accomplishments
- Professional development is supported
- Appreciation is expressed
- Employees connect with a sense of family or team
- Management accepts and supports employee's personal lives
- Employees receive unbiased feedback
- Opportunities to make a difference
- The company cares about the community, country and/or environment
- Differences are valued

**Note:** This list is not exhaustive. It was adapted from *Fortune Magazine* and *The Trust Model* from The Great Place to Work® Institute, Inc.

Ask yourself if you have an enriching home environment, one that will sustain you in the hard times. Note if your place of employment helps you sustain good health and the ability to bounce back. Take charge of your wellbeing by noting the ideas in the rest of this book that can support you into self-empowering action.

# III

# Demonstrations of Resilience at Work

## The Resilience-Generating Questions

IN preparation for this book, I interviewed women from all sectors of the work place. As well, 376 women from the audiences of 36 Canadian events participated in a survey. Dr. Al Siebert, author of *The Resiliency Advantage*, helped me formulate these three, key resilience-identifying questions:

- What is the worst work related experience you've endured?
- How did you cope?
- Looking back, describe what you learned.

Although this book focuses on activating resilience at work, the women's responses demonstrate the interweaving of resilience in all life arenas—home, family, community and work. For example, when a woman is in an abusive marriage, it affects her work. The consequences of distracted focus, absenteeism and lack of emotional containment are diminished performance, missed promotions, demotion—or worse—being fired. Conversely, if a woman comes home in a distressed state because of a crisis-driven, over-demanding and demeaning work environment, her family relationships become strained. For myriad reasons, too many women stay in soul-destroying relationships or toxic work environments...and so the circle goes round.

Consider also that women are typically socialized to be relationship-oriented and nurturers. This makes it difficult to compartmentalize job and home. Once we over-focus our time and energy in one place, that time and energy has to be drawn from somewhere else. Certainly, this reality was confirmed by the women I interviewed.

Many of the women's stories have similarities. Themes of adversity including unwelcome change, fear and distress are often repeated as are derogatory comments and challenges familiar to most women.

## Name Your Woes

Woe refers to internal barriers and workplace or home adversity experienced by survey respondents and interviewees. Think of "Woe is me!" with a big painful groan. Decide if your Woe or challenge is primarily internal (within you) or external (generated by someone else, your organization or a circumstance).

The degree of distress triggered by Woe situations may be intensifed by a lack of personal or external resources. Additionally, each Woe threatens one or more of the

## Maslow's Hierarchy of Needs

5. **Self Actualization**
   Life Purpose, Morals, Values and Integrity, Creativity, Potential
4. **Esteem or Self-Value**
   Confidence, Achievement, Self-Respect, Respect from Others
3. **Sense of Belonging**
   Giving and Receiving Intimacy, Affection and Care, Family, Friendships,
   Work Group, Community
2. **Sense of Safety**
   Protection, Security and Order
1. **Survival**
   Breath, Food and Water, Rest, Shelter and Clothing

   Adapted from *Motivation and Personality* by Abraham Maslow

levels described in Maslow's hierarchy of needs. Maslow concluded that we focus on higher-level needs only after lower level or basic needs are satisfied. Even then, if a lower-level need is temporarily not met or is in jeopardy, we will return there for attention and repair.

Woes might be usefully classified in two groups which I call internal Woes and external Woes.

## WOW-Empowered Women

Women are no longer damsels in distress; no longer perceiving themselves as victims; no longer begging "rescue me." They're asking themselves questions like: "What would Wonder Woman do?" "What would Hillary Clinton do?" What would my grandmother do if she had my education, knowledge, and freedom?" You have probably asked yourself the same kind of questions. So what do we tend to do when faced with adversity?

The *Woe to WOW Map* on the next page shows that sometimes we crash before we rise like a Phoenix from the ashes and get back on track. At other times, we face adversity head on and immediately put to use our WOW strategies and resilience tools. Sometimes our previous experiences have toughened us. Sometimes our internal hardiness supports us.

*WOW-Empowered women clearly ask for help and don't play victim.*

## Woe to WOW Map

This diagram illustrates the different reactions or responses women have when adversity strikes. Some have a high Woe resistance while others have a low Woe resistance. Regardless, most of us eventually use strategies to get back on track with our lives.

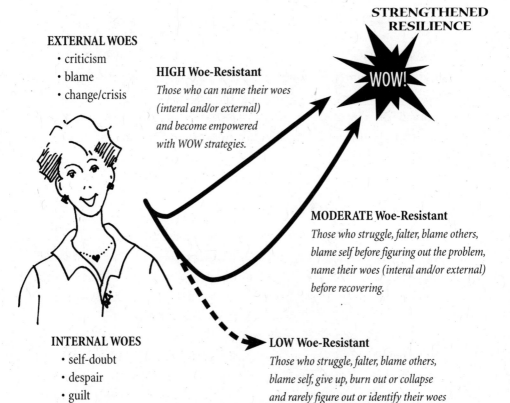

**STRENGTHENED RESILIENCE**

WOW!

**EXTERNAL WOES**
- criticism
- blame
- change/crisis

**HIGH Woe-Resistant**
*Those who can name their woes (interal and/or external) and become empowered with WOW strategies.*

**MODERATE Woe-Resistant**
*Those who struggle, falter, blame others, blame self before figuring out the problem, name their woes (interal and/or external) before recovering.*

**INTERNAL WOES**
- self-doubt
- despair
- guilt

**LOW Woe-Resistant**
*Those who struggle, falter, blame others, blame self, give up, burn out or collapse and rarely figure out or identify their woes (internal and/or external).*

## Internal Woes

*obstacles we tend to create*

1. Arrogance
2. Despair
3. Depression
4. Fear of abuse or more abuse
5. Fear of conflict
6. Fear of crying in public
7. Fear of rejection
8. Fear of losing a job
9. Fear of making a mistake
10. Fear of what others think
11. Fear of saying no
12. Focus on weaknesses
13. Guilt
14. Illness or disease
15. Ineffective communication
16. Lack of education and experience
17. Learning differences (disability)
18. Need to grieve
19. Negative self-talk
20. Over-achieving
21. Perfectionism
22. Passivity
23. Pessimism
24. Physical limitations
25. Self-blame
26. Self-doubt
27. Self-silencing
28. Victim mind-set
29. Workaholism
30. Worry

## External Woes

*obstacles others or circumstances create*

1. Blame
2. Bullying
3. Business betrayal
4. Caregiver demands
5. Change
6. Challenging co-workers
7. Conflict
8. Criticism
9. Difficult people
10. Discrimination
11. Emotional abuse
12. Focus on weaknesses
13. Ineffective communication
14. Ineffective management
15. Intolerance
16. Job termination
17. Lack of acknowledgement
18. Micro-management
19. Moral dilemma
20. Negative gossip
21. Sexism
22. Sexual harassment/assault
23. Solo parenting
24. Spousal betrayal
25. Stereotyping
26. Unchallenging work
27. Verbal abuse
28. Work/Home demands
29. Work overload
30. Workplace negativity

## WOW-Empowered Stories

*The power of story can inspire us to know and do better.*

### INTERNAL WOES

### 1. Self-Doubt

PSYCHOTHERAPIST Jack Rosenberg proposed that we have two basic and unconscious fears—being invaded or violated in some way and being rejected. Often, fear of rejection keeps us feeling insecure and reluctant to say *no*. Even those of us who are typically considered assertive can have off-guard moments.

*Talking to yourself is not a sign of craziness if your conversation is from your wisest self.*

SOLEIHA MAHRCELL loved her work as a professional server in high-end dining establishments. Given her restaurant experience and her managerial skills, a restaurant owner asked her to manage his two restaurants—to manage the staff, coordinate suppliers and oversee the financial and accounting operations of the business. Soleiha excelled at being in charge—delegating tasks, holding regular meetings and training her staff to be *in service*. She acknowledged and took into consideration the different demographics, the likes and dislikes of her clientele. Soleiha put in long hours on the job. Within a year, her boss expanded the number of restaurants to three. However, he ended up dissolving his partnership in the first restaurant and Soleiha became the Comptroller of the two remaining restaurants. The second restaurant was doing exceptionally well and ended up subsidizing the third—robbing Peter to pay Paul. Doing the accounts and receivables for both restaurants as well as the 20 daily server cash envelopes made Soleiha's workload time consuming and frustrating.

One day, Soleiha's boss asked her to walk to the bank with $40,000 in cash, even after she had mentioned to him the bank would not accept that much cash. The boss was adamant that they would take it and insisted that Soleiha walk to the bank with the bag of money. Typically, banks require business and fund transfer records when depositing large sums of money. When Soleiha arrived with her bag of money, the bank representative not only refused to deposit it, she called Soleiha's boss to say, "We don't feel comfortable having Soleiha walk back to the restaurant with this much money. Please send someone to accompany her back." Her boss refused. Soleiha recalls what happened when she returned to the office. "He didn't ask how I was but was only concerned that the money had not been deposited." The financial chaos continued to unravel with NSF checks, unpaid rent and not enough money to cover staff salaries. It escalated to the point when Soleiha's boss walked into her office one day, kicked her desk and yelled, "How dare you give the landlord the rent!" Soleiha knew she needed to quit her job.

Soleiha regrets violating her own boundaries, risking her own safety, working long hours and agreeing to carry around all that money. After she quit her job, she had an opportunity to re-examine her principles and concluded:

> You can't always act loving. Sometimes the most loving act is to stand in one's own sense of inner power and move on. Carrying that $40,000 to the bank was only one in a long list of acts that were out of alignment with my principles. I betrayed myself when I took on the management of another restaurant and when I put my health and my family relationships on hold while I worked nights and weekends. I knew inside that I was overcome by fear of rejection and fear of losing of my job. Still, I wish I had refused my boss's demands and said, No! The light-bulb moment came when I realized he wasn't going to change.

Not long after Soleiha quit, the second and third restaurants closed. The first restaurant, now owned solely by the former partner, was the only one left in operation.

Soleiha began a practice of getting in touch with how she feels internally before making a major decision. She checks to see if she feels any form of vulnerability, tapping particularly into any fear of rejection which might make her vulnerable to inappropriately pleasing others.

*Herstory Take-Aways:*
- Believe how people act rather than their talk.
- If it doesn't feel safe or right for you, don't do it.
- Remember you are not responsible for other people's businesses or life.
- Pay attention to your gut and trust your feelings.

*The Rest of Herstory:*

SOLEIHA MAHRCELL is now a sought-after marriage commissioner in Alberta, Canada. In her new role, she has come into synergy with her people skills of being in service and bringing out the best in people. Her new job is also in alignment with her spiritual practices. As she passionately says, "I'm there at the happiest moments in people's lives which gives my life a sense of joyful meaning."

## 2. Despair

WALK down any street in any city and you will see destitute people who have *despair* written on their foreheads. They have given up hope and lost all confidence. Stand around the water cooler in any office building and you will hear employees griping about the traffic, the weather or the stock market. They have lost their *joie de vivre*. Go into any bar and you will find the lovelorn lamenting their misery. They believe they will never be loved again.

Then there are WOW-Empowered women! Dozens and dozens of survey respondents reported adversity that could have *taken them under*—from being laid off to being bullied; from being verbally, physically or sexually assaulted; from grieving the loss of a loved one to being diagnosed with cancer. Even if they initially fell down, they eventually picked themselves up, dusted themselves off, and started all over again.

After the collapse of her *normal life*, JULIE DONNELLY never allowed herself to give up or give in. She was 41. Her children had left home and her 22-year marriage had ended. She was a prime candidate for depression, pessimism and hopelessness as she found herself alone for the first time in her life. She had little education, no money and no home. Rather than becoming despondent, Julie became resourceful. She slept in her car or on friends' couches. She applied for and landed a job with United Airlines at Kennedy Airport in New York. She describes her routine during those first few months of homelessness.

> Because I wouldn't always know where I would be sleeping, each morning I would pack a clean shirt, jeans, sweat shirt, pajamas, makeup and toothbrush into my yellow and white striped beach bag. I would arrive at work wearing my uniform. When I finished work, I would head over to a friend's house for the night. I would wash my dirty shirt and hang it up to dry and then iron the clean shirt so that I was ready for the next day's work. That's all I had—except for my car, all my possessions were in that beach bag. If a flight was delayed and I had to work late, I would sleep in my car and use the airport McDonald's washroom to get dressed and ready for work.

How did Julie manage against all odds to move ahead? Reading David Campbell's book, *If You Don't Know Where You're Going, You'll Probably End Up Somewhere Else*, helped her develop habits of optimistic thinking. She describes some of her approaches.

> I compartmentalized. When I was at work, I was at work. I could have felt really angry and upset. After all, here I was at age 41 with no material possessions. Instead, I pretended that I was 17 years old—the same age I was when I left home and married. At age 17, I thought the world offered unlimited possibilities. I didn't know that by getting married so young and by not getting an education, I was closing the door to endless possibilities. Now I had another chance. I started to think of myself as an intentional vagabond. I would ask myself, "What's going to happen today that is better than what happened yesterday?" I knew that whatever I focused on was going to become my reality. I thought of my cup as being half full and imagined what being completely full would look like. I began to image my ideal life.

Julie had always wanted to be a massage therapist. After working at United Airlines and then British Airways, she applied for a job at a travel agency. The regular hours made it possible for Julie to begin taking night courses and also gave her weekends free to study. After graduation, she landed a job working as a massage therapist on a cruise ship. She got to travel, she got to have fun and she no longer needed to worry about where she was going to sleep.

### Herstory Take-Aways:

- No matter your age, make the changes in your work and personal life that you desire.
- Allow yourself to think and act out of the box.
- Make yourself a smorgasbord of possibilities.
- Develop habits of optimistic thinking (See Julie's *Tips for Thinking Like an Optimist* on pages 108 – 109).

### The Rest of Herstory:

JULIE DONNELLY now lives in Spring, Texas. Even though she still loves to travel, she has a home and a successful career. She's an internationally recognized massage therapist, has developed a treatment for Carpal Tunnel Syndrome and is the author of *How To Be Pain-less... A Beginner's Guide to the Self-Treatment of Muscle Spasms*. She has also authored several published articles on the subject of Carpal Tunnel Syndrome. Along with her colleague, Dr. Zev Cohen, Julie Donnelly speaks at conventions, medical schools and health facilities across North America. To learn more about Julie and her work, go to <**http://www.julstro.com**>.

## 3. Guilt

WOMEN'S socialization to care for the babies, the sick and the vulnerable can become a set-up for us to feel guilt when we have two or more commitments pulling at us. We tend to invest in keeping everyone happy at work and home. I remember my mother's training in this regard. At social events, she would give me a plate of sweets and say something such as, "Now dear, make sure everyone is happy and has what they want." She trained me to be on the watch for others' needs, not to consider taking a sweet for myself until others were *happy* and not to question that my brothers were off playing and *being boys*.

> The mother's curse is believing, "If I really loved my child I would. . . (you fill in the blank)."

Twenty-eight survey respondents reported that their biggest workplace challenge was how home and family demands distracted them from job focus while an additional 13 said that the pull between home and workplace was their most significant challenge. Here are some of their comments:

- Difficult teen experimenting with alcohol and drugs and also has Attention Deficit Disorder (ADD). It's very challenging, stressful and time-consuming.
- The near loss of a child during the same time as losing our home.
- Husband's mother with Alzheimer's Disease takes a lot of my time.
- The relationship with my spouse is distressing.
- Our autistic adult son and teenager with Aspergers/Tourettes is a constant worry.
- My father is homeless with addiction problems.
- Blending families is difficult.
- Supporting my mother with breast cancer is emotionally hard.
- It was challenging placing my mother into a quality care home because of advancement of Alzheimer's.

And the list goes on. John Gray, in *Men are from Mars, Women are from Venus*, explains that men are apt (there are exceptions) to feel successful when they think they made their wife and children happy. Meanwhile, women tend to feel responsible for everyone's lives including their feelings.

One of LINDA BRADBURN'S most challenging experiences was when she daily left her three-month-old baby, Matt, with her parents in order to continue her teaching career. She had just received her permanent teaching certificate and her husband, Roy, was rising at 4:00 AM to do the chores on their new farm before driving to his day job at a General Motors factory. She felt like she was hanging on by a thread, asking herself, "Can we manage?"

Linda did manage. She stayed organized. She describes her strategy:

I knew what I'd wear the next day. I'd have the baby's items ready and packed. I would plan our meals. Since Roy and I had few hours to see each other, I left a lot of notes. It was like a long-distance relationship with him. I would call him from work. I'd get home and he'd be gone. The fact that we loved each other helped.

But feeling guilt was her biggest challenge. Although baby Matt was well cared for by his grandparents, every day Linda went to work feeling ashamed for leaving him behind. The belief that mothers *should* be home providing 24 hours of care to their babies haunted her.

> The worst part of leaving Matt was how I fantasized what other people were thinking, "She's leaving him for the *almighty dollar*." But I had put a lot of effort into my education and my salary was necessary if we wanted to keep the farm. It was a tug of war. "Should I stay home or should I go to work?" In the end, I'm glad I worked. At school, I focused on my job but there was always a picture of my son and, a few years later, my daughter on my desk.

Linda's WOW strategies included calling on her friends, asking for help and telling herself, "Kids are okay as long as they are with people who love them. Kids are resilient." But Linda has always used humor as a key strengthening tactic.

> I never really lost my sense of humor. I love kindergarten because the kids are so funny. They're so honest. I had a kid ask, "Do you love being a teacher?" "Yes," I answered and she said, "Well, I love being a kid." When I left one school, people wrote they enjoyed my laughter and humor.
>
> My humor is a gift from my mother. She doesn't mean to be funny. One day Mom said, "People in Blackstock must be drinking a lot of coffee. Almost every day I see the Percolator truck." She was seeing deliveries by the Purolator Courier. She's full of surprises and has taught me, if you can't laugh at yourself, you're in trouble.

### Herstory Take-Aways:

- Avoid letting what others might think haunt you.
- Minimize guilt as it can drain focus, energy and confidence.
- Take your work seriously and yourself lightly.
- A sense of humor is a useful coping tool.

### The Rest of Herstory:

LINDA BRADBURN has been a kindergarten teacher longer than she remembers, that is for nearly 30 years. Baby Matt and his younger sister are now adults. Roy and Linda enjoy evenings together at their farm house.

## 4. Workaholism

**B**ECAUSE women tend to readily accept home and work responsibilities, they need to be vigilant about avoiding workaholism. For our purposes we will define workaholism as a compulsion about working with little time devoted to personal relationships, rest and recreation, other than booking an annual pedicure. Workaholism just might be the core problem with a survey respondent who wrote, "I'm too busy, say *yes* too much, and have problems in my marriage."

*You are in trouble if you spend all weekend waiting for Monday.*

Arlie Hochschild, in *The Second Shift*, describes:

> Most women without children spend much more time than men on housework: with children, they devote more time to both housework and childcare. Just as there is a wage gap between men and women in the workplace, there is a "leisure gap" between them at home. Most women work one shift at the office or factory and a "second shift" at home.

However, single women may be even more susceptible to the *work-your-head-off* tendency. In *Married to the Job*, Ilene Philipson describes how the solo gal is vulnerable to lose sight of the rest of her life:

> Throughout history, women have married for economic survival and security. Thus, when women today marry their jobs, a similar logic applies. In a world of rapid economic change, family disintegration, and the ongoing expectation that it is women's responsibility to rear children; many, if not most, women look to the workplace for economic survival and security. Many are putting their hopes for fidelity and commitment through sickness and in health, for richer or poorer, in their employers. Jobs, not men, seem to offer more in the way of economic stability over the long haul.

SUZY WILKOFF'S story fits this description. She has a collection of awards and accomplishments from becoming the first and only female football recruiting coordinator at University of Miami, where she is an honorary alumni, to working her way up the ladder at Delta Air Lines where, in her twelve-plus-year career, she advanced from reservations to an outside sales representative position with a multi-million dollar territory. She left when she decided to move closer to her sister in Florida. After receiving heaps of job offers, she began working with one of the top golf instructors in the world. It was exciting driving around in a golf cart, working as an executive assistant. With the understanding that she would have to work some Saturdays but would have time off during the slow season, the hours increased and the money didn't; working six days a week and being paid for five. As she said, "I didn't mind working Saturdays but wanted to be compensated."

Between having high expectations for herself and living in Florida where employers can fire staff with no reason, Suzy allowed herself to work and work. She explains:

> I focused on the enjoyable parts of the job. I appreciated relationships with co-workers and customers. I tried to enjoy my personal time. I told myself, 'I'm organized. I'm tough. I don't cry. I don't pout. I don't complain. I can take a lot of stress and pressure.'

But Suzy also earned a reputation as a devoted, willing-to-do-anything employee. Working became her life. She left the job at the golf school and went on to another position with a corporation where she got into the same routine. She was not only performing her assignments, but was taking on those of some of the higher-level executives.

Then, one morning, Suzy woke up—in her forties and single. Although she had fun and joy in her personal life, she wanted a change. A wise perspective kicked in.

> The more work you do, the more work you will attract. You tend to give the message, "She can handle anything, willingly and enthusiastically." If you are like this and you do say *no*, it shocks people. Now, I'm a recovering workaholic.

It's hard to shift from investing twelve hours a day, six days a week to devoting some hours to your home and personal life. But Suzy did leave that job and began to re-prioritize her time, including engaging in leisure activities and starting a business helping clients become more organized.

### *Herstory Take-Aways:*

- Take advice from older and more experienced women.
- Do your best while having realistic expectations of yourself.
- Be honest with yourself and others.
- Avoid letting work consume your time, mind and soul.

- Create a bigger plan for yourself that includes pleasure, friends, family and self-care.

### The Rest of Herstory:

SUZY WILKOFF is the president and owner of Tasks Unlimited. She is the Founding President of the National Association of Professional Organizers, South Florida Chapter and spends ample time with friends, playing golf, walking, swimming and attending sports and cultural events, movies and parties. Learn about Suzy Wilkoff, Professional Organizer, and her work at <**www.tasksunlimited.com**>. See Suzy's *Tips for Avoiding Workaholism* on page 94.

## 5. Perfectionism

FIVE survey respondents described their worst work-related experience as making a mistake. A teacher's aide wrote, "When I kept on T.A. mode and a parent wanted to take her child home. I replayed the scene a hundred times and forgave myself, eventually." An office administer reported, "I sent an inappropriate email...It was difficult to reconcile and I internalized far too much." The fear of making mistakes is what drives perfectionism. A *Psychology Today* magazine article, "The Making of a Perfectionist," explains the beginnings of extreme fastidiousness. Some people grew up with parents who laid on constant pressure to achieve which in turn was heard as criticism for making mistakes. These parents repeatedly gave the message, 'You can do better,' regardless of how well done the chores or how high the report card marks. The negative impact of perfectionism includes:

It's hard living with a perfectionist, especially if it's you.

- Believing mistakes equal failure (rather than an opportunity to learn).
- Worrying about mistakes.
- Tendency to hide mistakes.
- Doubting one's ability to accomplish tasks.
- Minimal willingness to take risks.
- Reduced creativity and innovation.

The antidote to perfectionism is to understand the difference between excellence and perfection and to receive ample encouragement, appreciation and praise.

DONNA BARRY is a champion *perfectionist tamer*. As a manager, she loves to support her staff and helps them turn errors into learning. She has had a moment or two of embarrassing mistake making. She describes a moment of letting perfectionism interfere with her calm.

> When I was an assistant to a new vice-president of a manufacturing company, he asked if I knew PowerPoint®. I didn't but was afraid to admit it. I spent all afternoon developing a PowerPoint® presentation and then ended up losing the document because I had no idea how to save it. I looked for that PowerPoint® all afternoon and couldn't find it. He wrote in my employment review, 'One time lost a document.' I felt rather small.

But Donna learned to make PowerPoint® presentations with ease and moved on. She knows that fear of mistakes can diminish both confidence and productivity. When she became an office manager, she developed positive and loyal working relations with her staff through diligent, random and creative acknowledgment. If she didn't have the authority to give gifts, she'd bring flowers from her garden and put them on each person's desk. As she says:

> There are times employees need to be corrected but they can learn from their experience. When they fulfill a job, I let them know I noticed. I say things such as, "Thank you, You've come a long way," or "Sandy, I think you're doing a terrific job." People appreciate recognition.

Actually, the research indicates that employees flourish when acknowledged and are more apt to focus on excellence instead of perfection.

### *Herstory Take-Aways:*

- Learn to get over little errors and expect to work with ease.
- Discern between tasks that need to be just done from those that require high standards.
- Note when people are making an extra effort and encourage them.
- Give messages of appreciation verbally and in notes.

- Remember that a significant salary is nice but employees also need to feel appreciated for their contributions.

### The Rest of Herstory:

DONNA BARRY has an arrive-on-time habit as Sales Operation Administrator at 4Refuel Canada Ltd. She lives with her husband and looks on the bright side while surrounding herself with good female friends.

In 2007, 4Refuel Canada received seventh place ranking in Queen's University's *Best Employers in Canada* annual survey.

## 6. Physical Limitations

WHEN your body is wounded or ill, it takes total focus to mend. When your body is in crisis, it takes every bit of strength to keep motivated. If you are born with or develop long-term physical challenges, the associated difficulties can seem insurmountable.

*When the body yells for help, you'd better listen.*

A young, 30-year-old friend of mine, CHRISTIN SCHOLTEN, has worked as assistant to the producer of a number of films including *Bury my Heart at Wounded Knee*. What is astounding about this is the physical and health challenges that she has had to overcome. Christin was born with a damaged heart. At age three, she had open heart surgery. She was left with chronic congestive failure. At age five, Christin had a stroke which paralyzed the left side of her body. By age 14, she was diagnosed with scoliosis. Daily she experiences pain, shortness of breath and limited mobility and agility. But her passion for film overrides it all.

While Christin lives daily with physical limitations, most of us have to contend with an illness or injury now and then. At those times, we are required to attend to our physical well-being.

### The Rest of Herstory:

CHRISTIN SCHOLTEN is living her dream. She was accepted and is now studying at the American Film Institute Conservatory in Hollywood, California. She was one of 28 chosen from hundreds of applicants. She intends to produce movies featuring those who have been marginalized in our society. For more of her story, visit <**www.christin scholten.com**>.

~

A survey respondent wrote the following story:

> I had a farm accident with a tractor. I was injured and alone while taking care of 85
> head of cows. I phoned my husband who was working at the time in Egypt. I told him
> I was selling the cows if he was not coming home to help. He said that would be unwise.
> Four weeks later, he still hadn't shown up. I sold the cows.

Other women reported life-threatening illnesses like breast cancer and debilitating diseases like arthritis as their most physically challenging issues. Another woman said, "I have a blood-clotting disorder and recently lost my leg to Deep Vein Thrombosis. I am 29 and have a two-week-old baby."

The U.S. Bureau of Labor Statistics reported that workplace injuries and illnesses among private industry employers occurred at a rate of 4.4 cases per 100 full-time workers or 4.1 million Americans in 2006. Many times, unresolved workplace distress creates a break down in the body. A survey respondent wrote, "I was so miserable that I put my health in jeopardy." If you don't look after your body, you risk making a reality of the old adage, *If you don't have your health, you don't have anything.*

~

WOW-Empowered JANE is a senior vice-president of a national corporation. It took some effort and help from Jane's assistant to schedule our interview. When I finally spoke with her, I understood one of the reasons why scheduling was such a challenge. Jane had broken her knee and was unable to walk while the injury healed. For three months, she required the use of a wheelchair for long distances and crutches for short ones. Because of the accident and subsequent healing process, her productivity and typical pace of operation slowed down considerably. However, during our discussion, I realized how her injury was just another example of how Jane demonstrates resilience in the face of adversity.

We can only imagine the typical fast-paced day of this 50-something-year-old vice-president. During her recovery, Jane used the experience to learn some valuable lessons. She took responsibility for her own physical healing. She recognized her physical limitations, surrounded herself with those who would support her and told herself, "This won't last forever."

Jane learned the gracious art of requesting help from others and allowed herself to *lean on* others. At work, it was primarily her executive assistant and, at home, her husband. On reflection, she shared:

> I think a lot of women don't like to admit that they can't do it all. I say, "Pay for things to make life easier for you." That will keep you sane. Hire the best child care and forego your trip to Hawaii. Hire someone to clean. Order in a meal. Ask or pay for help.

She adds that what some call *stubbornness* can provide needed determination to overcome challenging situations. She says, "When adversity strikes, tell yourself that you will rise above this. Tell yourself to 'Just do it.'" She says she is often asked how she manages to juggle *it all*. She replies, "Just get started. Inactivity can get you down. Create a positive momentum and when you feel overwhelmed, focus on completing one thing." Jane says that the sense of accomplishment at completing even a small task allows us to move onto the next undertaking. "If your house is a mess, clean the bathroom. When you get that done, you can look back and see the difference."

She also believes that every experience can provide a lesson:

> I learned that it is sometimes essential to ask for assistance. The question is whether you apply what you've learned or not. It's important for us to ask, "Is this really going to matter in five years from now?" There are few real catastrophes. Almost everything can be fixed, reversed or learned from.

Jane's experience affirms, "This will pass."

### Herstory Take-Aways:
- Be willing to know when you are vulnerable and ask for help.
- Know that most setbacks are temporary.
- No matter how small or big the setback is, learn from the experience.
- When your body needs extra care, arrange it.

*The Rest of Herstory:*

JANE is mended, knows she's ready to handle the next challenge that comes through her door and is back in full swing attending to her executive responsibilities.

## 7. Learning Differences (Disability)

As a mother and grandmother of loved ones with disabilities, I have had a glimpse into the many challenges those with mental and physical restrictions face. Often, true ignorance (not really knowing) about the circumstances of those with disabilities limits the rest of us from cluing in and providing appropriate connection and help. Fortunately, we are becoming educated to the challenges, limitations and potential of those with visible and invisible disabilities. A section from the *United Nations Convention on the Rights of Persons with Disabilities* reads:

- Countries shall recognize that women and girls with disabilities are subject to multiple discrimination, and in this regard shall take measures to ensure the full and equal enjoyment by them of all human rights and fundamental freedoms.

- Countries shall take all appropriate measures to ensure the full development, advancement and empowerment of women, for the purpose of guaranteeing them the exercise and enjoyment of the human rights and fundamental freedoms set out in the present Convention.

KATHLEEN FASANELLA provides an inspiring example of not only overcoming a disability but using it for ultimate success. Kathleen's childhood was filled with physical abuse, judgment and neglect. She came from a family of morbidly obese people. By age nine, she weighed 150 pounds. As a teenager, she weighed close to 250 pounds. Her meek manner, detachment from others and avoidance of eye contact could easily have been explained by her obesity. Her ability to hyper-focus on tasks and her ability to shut out sights and sounds could easily have been explained as environmentally-conditioned behavior produced by her abusive

*It's not our limitations that count but how we use our abilities.*

childhood. Her shy demeanor, however, was primarily caused by a then little-known disorder called Autism.

With no help in coping with the disorder and little intervention to counteract her abusive home life, Kathleen left home, taking her 15-year-old sister with her. In order to support them both, Kathleen dropped out of school and got a job in a food factory working the third shift in the sanitation department. Kathleen started taking charge of her life in other areas as well. She bought a bicycle and lost more than 100 pounds over the next four years. Bolstered by that success, and acting on her best friend's mother's suggestion, Kathleen enrolled in the local community college to study pattern making. She graduated, got married and had a child. Unfortunately, by the time she was 25, Kathleen was a single mother. She was financially destitute with unpaid medical bills, no insurance, no child support, no vehicle and no place to live. Kathleen and her son sought refuge at a battered women's shelter.

As soon as they found a permanent place to live, Kathleen acquired a position in a garment factory. The job required intense concentration for extended periods of time. As her ability to shut out distracting noise became legendary, the only way to break through to her was to interrupt her directly. She believed most of these interactions were unproductive and a waste of company money. To reduce these interruptions (really attempts by other employees to socialize), she put a sign on her desk which read, "Don't interrupt me unless the building is on fire." One day, Kathleen was oblivious to the fire alarm. Her supervisor came to her wringing his hands and pleading with her to leave because the building really was on fire!

Unfortunately, the company was governed by fear—the fear of being fired. When a nearby Levi jeans plant announced its closing, the vice-president of Kathleen's company was giddy. He said, "There are 400 people who now need a job and x number of people who want *your* job." Kathleen describes her reaction. "At first, I bought into it. Fear was familiar and I was afraid. The fear was the same fear that I experienced when I was married and the same fear that I lived with as a child."

However, a moment of awakening happened for Kathleen. It was her *aha* moment.

When I was with my ex-husband, I believed anyone can be a victim. But actually, it's a choice. I chose not to remain a victim! I asked myself, "What's the worst thing that could happen to me?" The answer was, "I'd lose my job." It would have been easy to get into a negative spiral from there but the fact was I'd get another job. Analyzing my experience, I realized that I only went up in the face of adversity. I realized I never got worse jobs. In other words, the very best thing that could happen was to lose my job! In that instant, standing at my table, I was filled with a surge of happiness. I smiled, I laughed out loud. My entire life changed because I could no longer be controlled by fear.

Kathleen's confidence increased and she started to challenge the established company methodologies. As her suggestions were implemented, unit costs and defect rates decreased. After months of standing outside the plant at 6:30 AM waiting for the doors to open, she was finally given company keys. This allowed her to get in two hours of work without interruption before the rest of the staff arrived. It also allowed her flextime so she could be home when her son got home from school.

But the most significant day in Kathleen's life was the day she learned that she has autism. She calls it her *rebirth-date*. She began to understand and appreciate her gifts. With hyper-sensitivity and limited filters, she has uncanny capacities like smelling the sweat of a lie. Her razor focus gives her a productivity edge. She says, "First, I'm human. Second, I'm autistic. Third, I'm female."

Kathleen's message for younger women is, "Don't be afraid to make mistakes, fail frequently. Don't invest all your time and money in your looks and clothes. Invest in your brain. Read books, learn and grow. Start to live your dreams now." And one final word from a woman who ended up celebrating her different-ability: "We need to be more like us."

### Herstory Take-Aways:

- Exercise and eat well for optimum health and functioning.
- Transform feeling angry into positive action.
- Plan for the worst. Expect the best.
- Take calculated risks and challenge limiting rules.
- When possible find the ability in your dis-ability.
- Remember: Children can easily be victims. Adults typically have choices children don't have.
- Choose to not be a victim—pursue possibilities.

### The Rest of Herstory:

KATHLEEN FASANELLA is the author of *The Entrepreneur's Guide to Sewn Product Manufacturing* and is internationally respected in her field. She's married to a loving man, keeps a close eye on her son and is using her work experience to help others establish their own clothing lines and open their own factories. To learn more about Kathleen and her work, go to <**www.fashion-incubator.com**>.

## 8. Focus on Weaknesses

A Gallup Poll discovered that when people were asked, "Which will help you achieve greater success: building your strengths or fixing your weaknesses?" 59 percent of Americans chose *fixing your weaknesses*. Disappointingly, 62 percent of Canadian workers supported the weakness answer. Gallup Poll researcher and author, Marcus Buckingham, and other strengths-based proponents encourage *managing* our weaknesses while focusing on and developing our strengths as the means to create workplace satisfaction, improve employee engagement, increase productivity and bolster customer satisfaction. A useful saying is *maximize your strengths and minimize your weaknesses*.

*If you don't discover your strengths, who will? When you do, look out world!*

Think of how much easier our lives would be if, as children, we had been taught to really focus on our strengths. When our youngest daughter, Katie, was ten, she took a summer activity class in clowning. To everyone's surprise, Katie excelled at the art of balloon twisting, magic and storytelling. The summer program led to a character called Sassy the Clown who performed at lucrative and fun events throughout high school and university. As a professional clown, Katie was able to use her strengths to earn enough money to pay for her own education. Clowning helped Kate realize that her strengths were in working with children. Now, with a Degree in Education and a full-time position as a kindergarten teacher, Katie continues to maximize her strengths.

~

One survey respondent described her most challenging workplace experience as a job that, "Required me to do but not to think." Another reported, "I felt that my brain cells were wasting away. The job was not challenging enough and my skills and abilities were not fully tapped into." These women knew they had underutilized strengths but apparently did not know how to arrange for better-fit responsibilities. Here's a story of surviving and thriving by using strengths.

FAYE MCGHEE was a straight-A student in a Catholic school in a small community. By age 17, she was pregnant and married. Her small prairie community gathered 120 people to honor and support her future role as a mother and nurturer. That rural gesture provided a life-long lesson for Faye. "Regardless of age and circumstance, if we support other women, the best has a chance to come out. Despite my young age, I became a terrific mom."

Ten years later, at age 27, she landed her first job as a teacher's aide working with acting out and angry children. Surprisingly, many teachers in the school district were disgruntled with aides in *their* classrooms. Faye was assigned to a grade eight student with very troubling behavior who had experienced a series of abusive and neglectful situations. He was explosive, turned over desks and swore at those in authority.

Initially, Faye's presence in the school was largely ignored by the teaching staff and she was given little useful feedback. The message she did decipher was that teacher's aides were not needed or wanted. Faye describes the dilemma:

> Regardless of this challenging student's behavior, the teacher didn't want me to make contact with him. It was an attempt to prove that funding classroom assistants was unnecessary. She also believed that my involvement would have a detrimental effect on the whole classroom.

So Faye did her best under the circumstances:

> I sat and observed this young man, learning all I could about him. I interacted through body language. If he became very agitated in the classroom, I was allowed to walk down the hall with him. I used those times to develop our relationship.

Faye had a calming effect on the boy. She searched for his strengths, looked for the intention under his disruptive acts and appreciated him. She let him know she liked him. Eventually, she earned the trust of both the student and the classroom teacher. Faye truly believes that people will rise to their best when supported. With teacher and Faye in alignment, the student advanced to the point of interacting successfully with other children. Even more, Faye noted, "He first learned to trust me and then, as he trusted other adults, he was able to receive the academic and emotional support he so needed." The results were a cooperative student plus respect from teachers and the school principal. Faye clearly recognized she had strengths of observation, compassion and encouragement.

*Herstory Take-Aways:*
- Empower others when you can.
- Notice when you face challenges with ease.
- Identify and build on your and others' strengths.
- Look for opportunities where your strengths are used, appreciated and make a meaningful difference.

*The Rest of Herstory:*

FAYE MCGHEE attends to a variety of farming errands, is mother to five children and loves her work as a facilitator of Kneehill, Alberta and area community-building initiatives. She has taken her gift of empowering individuals and expanded it. She now empowers whole communities. She rallies citizens to become pro-active in establishing and maintaining programs such as Tools for Schools, youth engagement activities and family stabilization programs.

## 9. Lack of Education and Experience

WHILE some women appear content doing labor-related work, there are many others who are not. Some long to have more education and others couldn't care less. When I was in my last year of high school, my farming father told me that because I had three brothers he needed to keep any spare funds to support them through university. "You'll get married, have children and be supported. The boys need to have an education," he said. It's interesting that years later my husband encouraged me to take my first university class. At age 30, I felt both excited and terrified by the opportunity. Education does open up opportunities, options and often a door out of poverty and unsatisfying work.

*Learn who you are. Learn what you do well. Learn and keep learning.*

A survey respondent shared her perspective of having minimal education:

I know how hard it is to be a laborer. When I worked as a receiver in a warehouse, that kind of job in our country was called laborer; that is the work people in our country do who got no education.

Another woman wrote about her boss' unfair treatment. "I was treated as a non-person because I don't have a degree." Impressively, she stood up for herself. "I got together with co-workers and got the boss removed from the position. It is better to stick up for yourself…than be a doormat and be bullied. Working together and speaking up works!" You don't have to be stuck when you don't have a degree! When Oprah Winfrey says, "I think education is power," she could be referring to organized education *and* self-education—a willingness to learn about your passions, about your strengths and about the career path you want to pursue. Together, they are indeed powerful as Fedora knows.

~

FEDORA was a young woman when she fell in love with a Canadian and left her beautiful birthplace of St. Lucia in the Caribbean Islands. After her marriage failed, she found herself alone raising two daughters and working in unfavorable conditions, staying for fear of not finding better income. She describes her worst workplace adversity as, "putting up with anything. Men making sexual advances saying things like, 'you got a great butt,' asking me for dinner and giving me the eye." Fedora was the only woman working and operating a big machine in a certain area of a production factory.

They didn't care I was a young girl. I put up with it. I also put up with verbal abuse from a machinist. Whenever I told him the machine wasn't working, he'd yell, "Shut up!" and I'd worry he was going to hit me. Management would fire others before him 'cause he could fix machines.

Fedora explains how she coped with this day-after-day onslaught.

It was my only source of income. Smile, avoid conflict and try not to let it go any further. You put up with it so you can hold onto the job. I avoided working with him (the machinist) and would go to management instead of him to deal with problems. Every day I asked myself, "Today, am I going to be fired?"

Living in Canada, far away from family, was in itself terrifying for Fedora. No education. No financial or emotional support. No real relief.

I was always scared and afraid of what might happen to me and my kids. I'd ask myself, "Can I keep up with the rent? Keep clothes on my kids' backs?" Every day I'd tell myself, "You have two kids to feed." In everything, my two girls watched. I knew I needed a career. I needed to stop working where I was treated badly. I needed to do a job I was happy with because I would be a better person and mom to my girls.

With her educational barriers, the only jobs Fedora could successfully secure were domestic or factory positions. But when Fedora began focusing on a future career she began to notice some options. She noticed she had social skills. Many people came to her home for support and help regardless of how little she had. Sometimes she allowed herself to be taken advantage of but she knew she was trusted by many. She also knew how to use her hands. She wanted at one time to become accredited in cooking or hotel management.

Initially, hairstylist was not on her list as she was taught in her country of origin that it was "worthy of shame." But Fedora took another look. Social skills and working with her deft hands were a fit. Plus the requirements for hairstylist had lower demands than alternative careers while she raised her girls. Fedora describes her faltering steps towards succeeding to become a respected hairstylist.

The government loan pays for school but not the cost of living, so I had to keep working. I went to school eight in the morning until four in the afternoon then worked until eleven at night. I couldn't keep up with classes, looking after kids and working. I was always crying, never had enough money, was behind in bill payments and it was a stretch to even get food on the table. So after six months I dropped out.

But here's the real piece of resilience Fedora demonstrated. Following the disappointment and decision to curtail her training, she found a job as an assistant in a hair salon answering the phone, washing hair and doing a variety of tasks using her hands. She slowly took hairstylist courses and eventually completed her requirements.

How's it working for her? "I love being a hairstylist! I would be bored if I only had to do one task. If I only have one task to do, like in the factory, that isn't enough for me." Not only has the salon where Fedora works become the answer to her career and financial challenges but owner and staff have become like extended family for her and her girls.

*Herstory Take-Aways:*
- Make realistic career expectations that match your passions.
- Look at all the available options and try not to judge the possibilities.
- If you are an immigrant, accept that it's hard work adjusting to a new life in North America and get help where you can.
- You need a basic education for most satisfying career paths. Make that happen in whatever way works for you.
- To improve your education, access government programs while realizing you must do *the work*.

## The Rest of Herstory:

FEDORA broadly smiles as she cuts, colors and shapes hair at *Hairbiz* in Calgary, Alberta. She's a low-key gal who spends weekends cooking and hanging out with her teen girls and friends.

## 10. Self-Silencing

Two men were in a bar discussing their marital problems. One man said, "The other night my wife came to me on her hands and knees." His friend was impressed until the man explained. "Yep, and then she said, 'Get out from under the bed and face me like a man!'"

*Silence can be perceived as agreement. Is that what you want?*

Those who are addicted to being in charge often choose someone who lacks confidence or is financially or emotionally needy. Even though this issue is not gender-specific, it is often the male who is guilty of outwardly overbearing and controlling behavior. If you are on your hands and knees or metaphorically hiding under the bed, you have an abusive partner. If your main squeeze, parent, friend or boss tries to control you with criticism, judgment and self-esteem-eroding comments, you are in a toxic relationship. And if you believe you need someone to protect and care for you, the likelihood is that you will put up with this forceful and painful thumb on your head longer than any strong, confident and self-assured person would.

While some survey respondents described their most challenging time as their divorce, others described the distress of staying in a painful marriage. Indeed, a social worker wrote, "The worse experience I have endured is my relationship with my spouse." Domestic abuse (when one partner attempts to physically, psychologically or emotionally dominate the other) is still rampant in our society. When faced with controlling behavior, some people try to appease their partner or at a minimum stay silent. As it turns out, trying to keep the peace is not a wise choice.

Here is some telling information from a *New York Times* article:

A study (reported in *Psychosomatic Medicine*) of nearly 4,000 men and women from Framingham, Massachusetts asked whether they typically vented their feelings or kept quiet in arguments with their spouse. Notably, 32 percent of the men and 23 percent of the women said they typically bottled up their feelings during a marital spat.

In men, keeping quiet during a fight didn't have any measurable effect on health. But women who didn't speak their minds in those fights were four times as likely to die during the ten-year study period as women who always told their husbands how they felt. Other studies led by Dana Crowley Jack, a professor of interdisciplinary studies at Western Washington University, have linked the self-silencing trait to numerous psychological and physical health risks, including depression, eating disorders and heart disease.

As JOAN found out, *giving up on speaking up is giving up on yourself.* Joan was 19 years old when she married a man ten years her senior. He was already well established in the insurance and real estate business and he was already set in his ways. The first 15 years of the marriage was filled with raising their four children. Joan was an attentive wife, good mother and perfect daughter-in-law. As long as she looked after everyone else, all was peaceful and smooth.

The turning point in their marriage happened the day their youngest child started school. She got up that morning and asked, "Now what? What is it that I want to do?" She knew she wanted to work outside the home. Her husband thought otherwise. Against his wishes, Joan acquired her real estate license and later bought a travel agency. When she took action in directions that were personally fulfilling, her husband riled. She describes:

He was beside himself. He fought whatever I wanted to do. I actually borrowed money from my parents to buy the travel agency. I didn't need his approval to do this but it would have been nice to have his support. I could never come home and talk about my day. He repeatedly told me that I was a selfish person. He became increasingly verbally and emotionally abusive. He would throw his dirty laundry on the floor just to watch me pick it up. Anytime I started to talk about my business, he would silence me with, "Shush, I don't want to hear it."

Joan did her best to avoid confrontation. She threw herself into raising their children, running her business and building a supportive network of family and friends. During this period, she began to feel like an independent and successful woman, not just a wife, mother and daughter-in-law. As she said, "I was re-discovering myself."

The only time Joan's husband took an interest in her work was when it was to his benefit. As a member of the American Society of Travel Agencies, she had an opportunity to go to Rome. Of course, he was eager to accompany her but the verbal and emotional abuse continued and then escalated as soon as they returned home. The years of pretending and avoiding started to diminish her positive energy. After another ten years of being silenced, Joan's marriage ended.

"When my marriage ended, many asked, 'What was the problem?' The problem was that I could not be myself in the marriage. Most of my energy was spent in avoiding, covering up and pretending."

Once out of the marriage, Joan exercised even more personal freedom and returned to school. "Had I stayed married, I never would have received my Bachelors Degree in Business Administration and a Masters Degree in Public Administration."

Joan now encourages those choosing a partner to ask themselves, "Can you be yourself, your intelligent self, or do you have to be someone that person wants you to be?" She believes:

> We need to choose someone who helps us be our best. We need to find someone who enriches us and our life. First know yourself. Then know what you really want. Even if you are married and have children, have personal goals and seek to become personally fulfilled.

### *Herstory Take-Aways*:
- Hang onto your dreams and yourself.
- Choose your relationships carefully.
- Speak up!
- Create the life you want to realize.

### The Rest of Herstory:

For the past seven years, JOAN has been an instructor at a Community College in Hawaii teaching travel and tourism. She inspires confidence, self-respect and personal direction. Her students call her Teacher Mom.

## WOW-Empowered Stories

*The power of story can inspire us to know and do better.*

## EXTERNAL WOES

## 1. Criticism

THE Webster dictionary defines *criticism* as "an unfavorable comment or faultfinding." No one needs that in their In-Basket. Criticism can be the final act of unfairness in the long list of disrespect that people are willing to accept. In *Giving Notice*, Freada Kapor Klein writes:

> It is typically not the headline-grabbing incident that drives most women, people of color, and gays and lesbians out the door. Research conducted by the Level Playing Field Institute shows that the last straw is typically just another slight after an extended period of enduring daily micro-insults.

Sixteen survey respondents reported that criticism by managers wore on them. For ten of them it was the reason they left their positions. Here are some of their comments and circumstances:

- My department was short staffed and I was pulling double shifts and weekends. When I finally hired staff and could take a break, my boss told me I was *nickel and diming* him for time off.

- Having a past employer tell me in a review that I was expendable and not an important part of the team.
- I was reprimanded for asking for clarification but was also reprimanded when I did not.
- Boss saying I was unorganized and didn't know what I was doing!
- Was reprimanded in the lobby of a hospital for attending an educational session.
- Getting told I wasn't filling the expectations of my boss.
- A preceptor I had who was the manager of public health had mountains of negative feedback for me as a student nurse.

Many people actually fear criticism. Research cited in the book, *Driving Fear Out of the Workplace*, states:

At least 79 percent of all the people we talked with said that one of the reasons they had not spoken up in past situations was because they feared some type of repercussion. A workplace filled with finger pointing lowers morale and eventually catapults employees to the competition.

*Count on being criticized and trust yourself to deal with it.*

At one time, receiving criticism was a huge problem for JUDY ARNALL, one the most cheerful women I have ever met. In her early twenties, Judy was reconstructing her life while paying off a whack of debts from a failed marriage. While attending full-time classes to finish her schooling, she also worked full time as a receptionist for a social service agency. Her manager spewed buckets of criticism at her.

She was criticized for every aspect of her work—from how she answered the phone to how she typed letters. Her boss would regularly phone in to the office just to hear Judy answer the phone and then announce, "That sounds really bad." Sarcastic comments were written on letters she typed. When Judy divulged some of her problems—school, debt, divorce—the manager actively listened to them only to later use that information against her. The criticism increased when Judy began to use her lunch time for homework. Caustic notes were left on her desk. Her confidence and self-esteem waned. It was not just the manager who was critical and unsupportive. She learned that the female stereotype of backstabbing communicators is not unfounded. She began to believe that she was incapable of fulfilling the responsibilities of this job and would never be able to find another one.

To survive the manager's critiques and to overcome some of her own childhood insecurities, she began attending *Adult Children of Alcoholics, Emotions Anonymous* and *Overeaters Anonymous* groups. Those meetings got her through two years of being trodden on. Judy describes how she kept going back day after day. "I had supportive friends who allowed me to vent. I learned to laugh at my boss' critical micro-management. Going to school and getting good marks helped. I focused on where I was succeeding. I found the Serenity Prayer helpful."

Looking back, Judy says, "I wish I had the wisdom to know I would have been okay, even better off, had I left sooner. I'd tell younger women, 'Don't tolerate disrespect. No job is worth losing your self-respect.'"

The positive aspects of this negative situation were that Judy was motivated to seek support groups where she learned a menu of self-help strategies. Judy did eventually leave that company. "My next job was at a company where the communication was direct and honest. Issues were resolved and criticism was constructive rather than destructive."

### *Herstory Take-Aways:*
- Acknowledge that you are more important than a toxic job.
- Consider joining a self-help group.
- Filter criticism.
- Learn to focus on your strengths and celebrate your successes.
- Memorize the Serenity Prayer:
  *God grant me the serenity to accept what I cannot change,*
  *the courage to change what I can, and the wisdom to know the difference.*

### *The Rest of Herstory:*
JUDY ARNALL met her second hubby while volunteering on a crisis line. Judy home schools their five children, is a contest-winning Toastmaster, nationally recognized parenting expert and the author of the critically acclaimed book, *Discipline without Distress: 135 Tools for Raising Caring, Responsible Children without Time-Out, Spanking, Punishment or Bribery*. To learn more about Judy and her work, visit her website at <**www. professionalparenting.ca**>.

## 2. Blame

A store cashier reported in the survey that she cried in her basement suite for a month after a blaming incident. She was, "accused of stealing when she didn't have training on the cash register." She never stole a cent but was unable to balance the cash at the end of the evening. She quit her job but never recovered from the incident. Unfortunately, people have a tendency to either blame themselves or blame others. Those who *blame own* will accept responsibility for almost anything that goes wrong while those, such as the cashier's boss, *blame throw* by faulting others. In both cases, the knee-jerk question of, "Who's to blame?" is best replaced with, "What's the problem and how can we solve it?"

*Darn! At work you can't get away with blaming the dog.*

**BEVERLY FALKEID** became a WOW-Empowered woman after she had the nasty experience of being falsely blamed. She had always dreamed of travel but as a single-parent mom did not have the time or finances to do so. When her son left home, she applied and was hired to teach English in Japan. While she enjoyed interacting with the children and their families, working with the school's administration was a different story.

Conflict began almost immediately with her ex-pat Canadian boss. Every week he called her *on the carpet* for something. When she was contacted by him at her school one afternoon, she expected to be reprimanded once again. But this time the accusations were more serious. She was accused of not participating as a respectful team player. She explains:

> My manager expected me to answer calls from him any time of the day, any day of the week. Taking job-related calls on my days off seemed unfair. On this latest incident, my boss was particularly angry because he thought I hung up on him.

Actually, Beverly's cell phone battery had died and the conversation ended midstream. She was unable to phone him back but it didn't matter. The boss was unwilling to accept her explanation and unable to excuse her. Beverly was told to meet with her boss and his supervisor, who was the regional manager, at 8:30 the next morning.

That night, Beverly could not sleep. She felt scared and alone. She made a phone call to Canada to access support. Actually, she called me. She realized she could easily react in defensiveness, make counter attacks and complain about her unreasonable boss. However, she wanted to continue working for this organization and she needed a strategy that would project a calm and rational manner. We put a plan in place to keep her feeling confident throughout the meeting. Here is a summary of her plan:

1. **Take a symbol of love. In one hand hold a stone or small object that has personal meaning**: It's like an anchor. Beverly had just been given a small dog charm by one of her students. She held onto that tiny dog charm through the whole interview. At the end, she returned it safely to her pocket.

2. **Develop an assertive line or two to say over and over**: Beverly used, "I think we've had a misunderstanding" and "I have done my best." She used these each time her boss accused her of wrongdoing. Not once did she counterattack or state anything negative.

3. **Look at the most kind and supportive face. Breathe in the feeling of support**: The regional manager who also was an ex-pat Canadian was the most supportive of her during all the allegations. There was a brief flicker in his eye when he returned alone for the final talk. In that millisecond, Beverly knew she had succeeded. She knew that he knew she was unfairly treated. The tide had turned.

4. **When appropriate, ask how you can meet the other's underlying need**: Beverly asked, "What do you suggest I do?" and "What do you suggest I do differently?" Both Beverly's boss and the regional manager indicated approval of these questions. Her boss seemed to calm as his position and status was acknowledged. Furthermore, these questions required him to explain how she could improve her performance and forced him to justify his allegations.

Beverly's plan worked. She was steady throughout the difficult meeting. Later, when I interviewed Beverly about this incident, she confirmed that not only had she recovered from unfounded accusations, she also affirmed her own strength and abilities. She felt fear yet stood her ground.

I had to accept that people will live and act according to their own experiences and issues. I had to be prepared for others to let me down and disappoint me but I also had to have a plan. I realize now that it comes down to choosing my actions and reactions.

With a laugh she added, "Darn! I had to develop both an attitude of self-acceptance for my imperfections as well as develop resiliency to overcome the accusations of imperfection."

### *Herstory Take-Aways*:

- Reach out for support.
- Feel the fear and take action to look after yourself.
- Breathe.
- Speak respectfully and expect to be treated likewise.
- Seek mutual agreement.

### *The Rest of Herstory*:

**BEVERLY FALKEID** is back in Canada, reconnected to family and friends and working as a Recreational Therapist. She says:

While traveling through Asia, I met many wonderful people and had amazing experiences. I did leave that first job and moved to another company and location in Japan where I had a supportive group of co-workers and employer. Before I returned to Canada, the whole school gave me a wonderful goodbye.

She came back a stronger and wiser woman.

## 3. Verbal Abuse/Bullying

VERBAL abuse can include harassment, discrimination, sexism, put downs, swearing and off-the-Richter-Scale yelling. Unlike criticism which typically focuses on behavior, verbal abuse is often demeaning language that attacks self worth. In the book, *You Can't Talk to Me That Way! Stopping Toxic Language in the Workplace*, business coach, Dr. Arthur Bell, describes verbal abuse as:

- Focused on who we are, not what we do…"You're a liar."
- Focused on inflicting pain, not on expressing emotion.

- Playing on vulnerabilities in a way that discourages constructive change.
- Out of proportion to any reasonable communication for a given situation.
- Often accompanied by a violent, memorable act or gesture.

*Verbal Abuse: What they say to you might not be any of your business.*

Fifty-four survey respondents reported either verbal abuse or bullying (which typically includes verbal demeaning) as their worst workplace experience. The majority of this onslaught came from managers, then clients or patients and least from co-workers. Disappointingly, I read stories of women in the so-called *caring professions* tolerating verbal abuse from their directors. One helping professional reported that her boss would bang on the desk and yell, "I'm in charge" and to the whole staff yell, "F#$@! You don't listen to a F#$@ word I say." She said that she watched good people get fired and now wished that she had stood up for them. Women in the helping professions are also susceptible to verbal abuse from clients such as troubled teens and those with mental health issues.

Surveys by health researchers, Helen Cox and Laura Sofield, discovered that more than 90 percent of nurses surveyed had experienced verbal abuse and most encountered an average of five incidents per month. Indeed, many health organizations, of all places, are *sick* with inexcusable behaviors. A nurse and survey respondent described her worst work experience as when "a surgeon threw a scalpel across the room in the operating room." Another nurse reported that she endured "ten years of total harassment from a psychotic and jealous manager."

CHERYL WEAVER faced verbal abuse that crossed the line of civility and included foul language, blocks to resolution and unreasonable demands. Amazingly, she learned to *manage* her verbally abusive boss.

Cheryl is a woman confident in her accomplishments. Some of that confidence was developed when, as a marketer in Hawaii, she worked for a very intelligent but manipulative CEO. With a lack of people skills, the CEO ranted and raved with demeaning comments about his employees and colleagues. After unloading his frustrations to Cheryl, he'd say, "It's a F@#@ mess. Go tell John this." Apparently, one sub-cultural phenomenon in Hawaii is a tendency for men to avoid confrontation with other men. Hence, women often find themselves in the middle or completely ostracized.

No matter how intimated Cheryl felt, she stood up to him. Previously, when Cheryl had worked at California Coast Credit Union in San Diego, she learned an effective policy and philosophy. All employees were given a button that read *I own it!*—meaning *don't pass the buck*, or own your part in situations or problems (bad, good or ugly) and don't blame someone else.

Rather than back down from her boss, Cheryl faced him head on. "As uncomfortable as it could be, I would approach him with professionalism and a sense of self-worth, that I was valuable to the senior management team and the company."

Cheryl learned to analyze working styles and personalities, to improve her communication skills and to provide analytically oriented co-workers and supervisors with data to make her point. As she advises, "Work on your approach before squaring off."

### Herstory Take-Aways:

- Know your own worth.
- Acknowledge others.
- Seek to understand others *before taking them on*.
- Stand your ground.
- Take responsibility for your part in problems. *"I own it!"*

### The Rest of Herstory:

CHERYL WEAVER is the Operations Manager for Kamehameha Federal Credit Union in Hawaii. She enjoys hiking and golf with her close circle of friends. Her message to younger women is, "Be true to yourself." Her motto is, *"With rain there's always a rainbow."*

~

The majority of survey participants who reported being bullied indicated that it came from those in management positions and that sooner or later they left their positions. One wrote, "I had an employer who was over-controlling, non-trusting, constantly insulting and putting us down." Five women described co-workers as bullying them. Bullying also troubles bystanders. "I witnessed workplace bullying. The woman being bullied became very ill and I still believe there was a connection."

It is important to discern between immature behavior or poor communication skills and bullying. In *Bully Free at Work*, author, Valerie Cade, defines *bullying* as, "repeated, deliberate, disrespectful behavior by one or more people toward another for

*Bullying: Imagine the temper tantrum played out, not in a business suit, but in diapers.*

their own gratification, which harms the target." Bullying is not only a source of emotional and physical illness but high employee turnover, reduced productivity, lower morale, increased absenteeism, stress leave and even Post Traumatic Stress Disorder. Going to work where a bully operates is scary.

The facts are rampant. An American Institute of Stress report indicated that 19 percent of employees said bullying happened in their workplace in the last year. In the meantime, The Workplace Bullying Institute's Zogby Survey reported that 37 percent of American workers are bullied with an additional 12 percent witnessing it. According to a survey in 2000 conducted by Drs. Ruth and Gary Namie of the Workplace Bullying Institute:

- Forty-one percent of those targeted by bullies were diagnosed with depression.
- Women comprise 58 percent of the perpetrator pool, while men represent 42 percent.
- Overall, 80 percent of individuals targeted by both male and female bullies are women.

SUSANA SLAVNIK had a first-rate lesson in dealing with bully-like behavior. When in a support role for a corporate training business, she noticed that her boss's tirades not only wore on her but others as well. As she said, "I realized, this isn't just me. It affects everybody." It was not uncommon to be yelled at with "You have to stop this! You can't! I said right now!" and "Don't you ever get in my F#$@ way! You make me crazy!"

Susana began to study the phenomenon of workplace bullying. She learned that those with bullying tendencies:

- Misrepresent facts to superiors.
- Lie about co-workers.
- Take credit for others' ideas and accomplishments.
- Give little or no credit to those who legitimately earned it.
- Block others from doing their work.
- Control the budget.

- Grandstand at meetings by finger pointing and using confrontational and controlling language.

To protect herself, her job and her sense of self-worth, Susana arranged for coaching, learned to ask powerful questions, created a support network and enrolled in courses such as conflict resolution, assertiveness, appreciative inquiry and personality and behavioral assessments (DISC and Myers Briggs Indicator). She learned that some people who act aggressively are bullies while others are simply poor communicators.

Then she put her knowledge with her aggressive boss to the test. She arranged for one-to-one conversations, invited questions of introspection and talked to mentors. She recognized that those with intimidating tendencies don't take responsibly for their abusiveness—for what they do, say and how they say it. She discovered her boss lacked effective communication skills more than he was a classic bully.

Susana advises:

Surround yourself with people who act with respect and dignity and help you get done what you need to get done. Confront sooner than later. Use phrases such as, "I'm uncomfortable with the tone you are using" or "If you prefer, we can reschedule this meeting." Don't over explain your position to the attacker and don't defend your position. And don't ever go on the bully road yourself. Always be able to defend your position, the work you have done—bullies are always on the lookout for weaknesses and will use this to their advantage and your disadvantage. My most resilient technique is reminding myself to always take the high road.

### *Herstory Take-Aways:*
- Name the harmful behavior.
- Have clear boundaries based on your value system.
- Stand up for yourself.
- Confront sooner than later.
- Learn assertiveness skills.
- Expect and require respect from others, no matter their position.

*The Rest of Herstory:*
With an MBA, SUSANA SLAVNIK is the Manager, Institutional and Analysis Projects at Southern Alberta Institute of Technology. She is devoted to her young family and her community. She is described by Frances Wright, the founder of the *Famous 5 Foundation*, as a "fabulous volunteer."

## 4. Sexual Harassment/Assault

SEXUAL comments and advances can be expected when men and women work together. This is not a problem if the comments and advances are welcome and the boundaries around conflict of interest are observed. The problem occurs when the approaches are unwanted, abusive or exploitative. The term *sexual harassment* includes unwelcome sexual advances and pressure for sexual favors connected to an individual's employment. Here are some figures from *The Sexual Harassment Handbook*:

- A typical Fortune 500 Company loses $6.7 million per year in absenteeism, low productivity and employee turnover due to sexual harassment.
- One of every two sexual harassers is the victim's supervisor.
- Nine out of every ten sexually-harassed women suffer from debilitating stress reactions, including depression, headaches and other physical symptoms.

Survey respondents reported a number of crude and rude comments and direct advances made to them by their bosses:

- A boss who constantly remarked on my weight. Every day he made comments about my hips, butt and boobs.
- Boss insulted me using sexual-harassing terms at the coffee machine in front of co-workers.
- At my first job the boss made sexual advances.
- The school principal hit on me over and over.
- "Hey baby! Come sit on my face."

Two respondents reported sexual harassment from colleagues while another reported sexual assault from a co-worker. Although sexual harassment can put a woman's mental health at risk, sexual assault can be even more debilitating.

*Women need martial arts alertness in domineering testosterone territory.*

When GESA HARMSTON was a child, her parents raised her with their values as Peace and Human Rights Activists. By the time she had completed high school, Gesa had seen a lot of the world and felt well equipped to travel on her own. She set off to live and work in Australia. As a fruit and vegetable-picking laborer, she endured poor working conditions, long hours and corruption. Her childhood experiences, however, fueled a desire to live and work in cultures where English was not the native language. At 22 years of age, she traveled to northern Peru to teach English.

Early one evening, while strolling on Mancora Beach, a young male physically attacked her. It was clear that his intention was to sexually attack her as well. Male dominance is more prevalent in Peruvian society and Gesa feared that, even if she screamed, no one would come to her aid. She remained silent as she wrestled her foe. When she could not escape, Gesa took a risk and screamed. Miraculously, people came to her rescue. But then Gesa took another risk. Even though she doubted the police would take action, she reported the incident. Gesa later discovered that three other women in the village had been assaulted. After Gesa reported the attack, the other women came forward. The assailant was arrested and put in prison. When he was released after only two months of imprisonment, the villagers shunned him.

Gesa, however, was faced with a dilemma. With world-street wisdom, she considered her situation: "Do I stay in this village or do I retreat to a safer environment?' She decided to stay. She said:

> I thought that I could best release the fear and negative energy by staying. It's easy to doubt, get sidetracked or get distracted. By staying, I didn't let his attack ruin my experience or my passion to work with these incredible people.

Stubborn, strong minded and determined are attributes that kept Gesa walking through her scare. She also practiced a visualization process to keep herself centered. She says, "Sometimes I cleared my energy points, my seven main chakras. Sometimes I wrote. Sometimes I danced."

Ultimately, Gesa trusted herself: "When I really believe in something, I won't give up." Gesa stayed and taught in the community for a year.

*Herstory Take-Aways:*

- Use your brain to keep yourself safe. Never walk alone at night.
- When in danger, yell for help and fight for your life.
- Face your fear rather than sit in it.
- Share your story without shame.
- Rise above negative experiences.

### *The Rest of Herstory:*

GESA HARMSTON worked as a youth leader and mentor for Ghost River Rediscovery, a non-profit organization focused on Aboriginal Youth Leadership. GRR receives funding from CIDA as well as from many other sources. She is now a certified Life Coach as well as an International Travel Advisor for an organization in Ottawa, Ontario.

## 5. Sexism

AN unsettling in our stomach happens when subtle sexism occurs. It's just that —subtle. Business author, George Fuller, describes it like this:

> Their (women's) male counterparts may follow the letter of the law in terms of actionable discrimination, yet ignore the spirit of the law by their actions. For example, a female worker in a predominantly male environment may find her recommendations being ignored or belittled. She may also find herself being socially ostracized by not being invited to lunch and other business-related functions.

Regardless of the subtleness, this kind of workplace mistreatment needs to be recognized and addressed. If not, you may repeatedly end up in losing situations, be looked over for promotions and start to wonder about your sanity. The trades are rampant with subtle and not so subtle forms of sexism. Just ask Bonnie Amundson.

BONNIE BAKKUM AMUNDSON was the first woman to graduate from her college in construction management (1976) and the first woman to work on a construction site as a union glazier in the mid-western US. Glaziers are responsible for preparing large window openings in new buildings under construction and for installing the glass. Like *Cat Woman*, she was quite the daredevil sight—five feet, two inches high with a safety belt around her waist, hooked to a cable as she leaned outward into the

*Subtle Sexism: The trades can be a tricky place for women to show they're stronger than they look.*

four by six foot openings on every floor of the 49-storey Minneapolis City Center Building. On another job, she worked from the outside on scaffolding and discovered that men often feel intimidated when a strong woman works alongside them. "There were guys on the inside of the window mimicking me as I worked on the outside completing the installation of the glass."

It wasn't just the guys on the construction sites that showed signs of *subtle sexism*. She worked for a manager who tried to detour her into clerical work by explaining that it was "a good opportunity." Notice the *subtle sexism*. After she declined, the manager increased her workload without pay compensation and avoided clear communication. Conversations that began with "Do you want to?" ended with "That's insubordination." Again notice the *subtle sexism*. Bonnie learned that those who identify themselves as "The Boss" are not always leaders. They often use intimidation to manage.

She learned a lot about *equal opportunity* programs: "It's not about being a woman or of a certain race. I've experienced equal opportunity bosses who are jerks to everyone, not just women or visible minorities. Insecurity, ego and greed create problems." Bonnie concluded that titles don't make leaders and that organizations with high productivity have managers who demonstrate respectfulness.

Bonnie's main WOW strategy is to connect with different friends for different reasons. Her friends helped her tough through the hard days of feeling frustrated with sexism and provided valuable support. Anita, a friend since grade school days and a phone call away, still provides *head talk*. Like deep psychotherapy, time with Anita includes crying, going deep into an issue and laughter. Bonnie's *work friends* are not privy to these vulnerabilities. Bonnie notes, "In a work environment, I don't share work concerns. The person you're asking to listen and help can become distressed by the situation."

Other supportive friendships include what Bonnie calls *The Ya-Ya Sisters*, a trainer from her gym and a woman who works with special needs children. They provide Bonnie with companionship, listening and encouragement like, "You go, girl!" Professional friends, like her friend who is a lawyer, offer Bonnie expert information. *Truth-telling* friends tell what others won't risk (anger or rejection) and *men friends* provide a practical and objective male perspective. In Bonnie's categories, only *friends of convenience* are to be avoided—those people who come around when they need something without a spirit of reciprocity.

### Herstory Take-Aways:

- Don't allow your gender to determine your career path or your value.
- Clear the path as a strong woman so others can follow.
- Create a friendship circle to remind you of and sustain you in your womanpower.
- Develop a variety of friendships.

### The Rest of Herstory:

BONNIE BAKKUM AMUNDSON went back to school and is now a Certified Master Life Coach focused on Corporate Culture and Transition. Her mission is to energize and champion companies and every employee within those companies because she believes in decency and wellness in the workplace, leading to win-win situations for all involved. To learn more about Bonnie and her work, go to <**www.amundsonlife construction. com**>.

~

> *Blatant Sexism: she didn't let his stereotyping "sink" her.*

A hard-to-place, unemployed man walked into my office. As I offered a handshake, he exclaimed, "You're a F#$@ woman!" In spite of the statement being redundant, I was taken aback. Call it stereotyping. Call it sexism. It's still around and tripping up women's careers.

The Merriam-Webster dictionary defines *sexism* as, "prejudice or discrimination based on sex; especially discrimination against women." A survey respondent and purchasing coordinator described her experience. "I was told that I would not be accepted for the position because women couldn't cut it." According to workplace commentator, Harriet Rubin, 52 percent of middle management employees in North America are currently women. How then can sexism persist? In *Why Men Earn More*, Warren Farrell shares some statistics from the Gallup Organization:

People in 22 first-world countries were asked, "If you were taking a new job and had your choice of a boss (supervisor), would you prefer to work for a man or woman?"

- Forty-seven percent of men preferred men as bosses and 14 percent preferred women as bosses.
- Forty-seven percent of women also preferred men as bosses, while 21 percent preferred women as bosses.
- Twenty-eighty percent did not care one way or the other.

So discrimination against women can be attributed to both sexes. Go figure!

LINDA GINAC was a WOW-Empowered woman extraordinaire who experienced discrimination, not only because of her gender, but also because she was married. Linda was Vice-President for Product Strategy, the only female executive for a company with about 250 employees. Because of a merger, layoffs of 75 people were required. The executive team began discussing downsizing strategies. Linda describes the process.

The night before the discussions were to begin, I couldn't sleep. Like a princess lying on a pea, I was restless. I went into work early and saw cars in the parking lot. At that time of day, the parking lot was usually empty. I went into my office and then walked past the boardroom. Every company executive except me was there. The CEO came out into the hallway and said, 'We're going to have another layoff and I think you should be on the list. We think it should be you because, even though you are the brightest, you have a husband.' In my head, I thought, 'How dare you say that?'

But her years as an executive overruled her thoughts and she refused to show her vulnerability or let them "know they've got me." She only asked, "When do you want this to happen?" She was given 30 days to pack up her desk.

She shares what happened when she got home. "Of course, I cried. I consoled myself by thinking, 'I am totally equal *but*, if this is the way the company treats women, do I really want to work for them?'"

Linda's greatest resilience-strengthening strategy is nurturing a strong and healthy marriage and family life. She describes *her Frank* as highly supportive, loyal, honest, stable, thoughtful and encouraging. She also describes their relationship as two lives intertwined—a pair of opposites who care, share and bring one another up from the inevitable slumps. She elaborates, "I had a tough upbringing and he is my rock. People see me as an assertive and confident person because he helped me develop my self-esteem." Indeed Linda was raised in a family surrounded by addiction-related dysfunction. By the time she was 16 years of age, she was in her own apartment wondering how to pay the heat bill. She moved from surviving to thriving to creating a fulfilling life with Frank.

Although Linda describes herself as being opposite to Frank, they share many values. They make room on their calendar for half marathons in support of a cure for cancer, plan both a weekly family night with their children and a weekly night for friends, and have their own date night most Saturdays. In addition, they take two formal family vacations and three couple only mini-trips each year. Linda explains all this pre-planning:

> When you're married, you shouldn't have a desire to hang out clubbing. Sure, we have different groups of friends and different groups of people who like to hang out with us. But you need to plan couple time or it won't happen. Our Saturday night dates and mini-vacations help maintain our marital equilibrium. We also do things spontaneously. Do we plan intimacy? No. That happens spontaneously.

Oooh, don't we all wish we had a Frank?

### Herstory Take-Aways:
- Stay steady and take the high road if and when faced with sexism.
- Partner with someone who celebrates your intelligence, passion for work and is not intimated by your successes.
- Once you have a healthy relationship, make it a priority with your time, energy and focus.

### The Rest of Herstory:
LINDA GINAC is the primary owner of The Ginac Group Inc., a firm that trains and certifies career coaches. In addition to being a tri-athlete and marathon runner, she also practices yoga. Her husband and children continue to be her top priority. Linda was chosen one of the top five most powerful women in Central Texas. To learn more, go to <**www.ginacgroup. com**>.

## 6. Intolerance

I'LL never forget the moment I was told it was hard to place me as a professional speaker because I was an older woman. Older! Woman! How can I change those facts? Aren't there advantages to who I am? Different is too often discriminated against. Isn't it fascinating that women are viewed as different in the workplace and the world when we're 51 percent of the population? Add to this strange phenomenon additional differences such as race, economics, disabilities, personality, sexual preference, physical appearance, weight, size or shape and you may be a target for repeated discrimination, disrespect and unfairness. Hubert Herring reported in *The New York Times* the following:

> *Think of "weird" as "have found your own way." Celebrate it.*

A 2005 survey of 623 employed Americans found that, 30 percent of those surveyed said they overheard racial slurs, 20 percent reported ridicule of sexual orientation and 20 percent were privy to age bias during the previous 12 months.

Many women do what they can to escape intolerance from others and themselves. Think of Botox, breast implants and liposuction. Every day, countless women cause pain to themselves in search of the culturally defined *beauty normal*. In seeking *normal*, they strive to become skinnier or fatter, curvier or flatter, darker or lighter or brighter. Actually defining *normal* is a futile pursuit. For those looking for normal, it's on your dryer between cold and hot.

Other than appearance, there are many ways to be different. Workplace tolerance policies are often not good enough. Who wants to be merely tolerated? Merely allowed to exist? Not Roxy Anderson.

When 40-something-year-old **Roxy Anderson** began working on construction sites, her male co-workers thought she couldn't do the job. Each work day she drives an average of 200 kilometers (120 miles) through construction zones to deliver plumbing supplies—copper tubes four inches wide and 10 feet long weighing between 50 and 60 pounds each. Sometimes she delivers toilet tanks and bowls that weigh, on average, 50 pounds. The construction site grounds are often uneven with rocks, gravel and, on rainy days, mud. Sometimes there's an extra pair of willing and helpful hands to help unload the truck; other times, the workers sit and watch the *Roxy show*.

Roxy describes establishing herself:

> When I started, I had to prove I could do it. I was delivering 150-pound shower stalls and 300-pound water tanks. You learn how to move and not hurt yourself. I have had plumbers say in amazement, "You took that off yourself?"

She also had to deal with sexual harassment and discrimination. Fortunately, her company has a code of ethics which includes no harassment. Every employee is required to annually read and sign the code. If there is coarse language, Roxy mostly ignores it. Sometimes she tells them, "I don't need to hear that kind of language." They'll say, "I'm sorry. I didn't know you were there."

One day during a delivery, Roxy offered to help a client.

> The client said, "No, I will use my workers to do it." He added an insulting racial slur when referring to his staff. I was in shock. When I reported the incident, my supervisor immediately cancelled all contracts with that company. I was glad I worked for an ethical company.

Another day, a co-worker and Roxy were delivering a hot water tank. She overheard him say to another co-worker, "If she lost some weight, she wouldn't sweat so much." Once again, her company acted immediately requiring an apology for the disparaging remark.

> Over the years, I've learned to speak up and say what's acceptable and what is not. That's important to me on the job but also important on a personal level. As a survivor of childhood sexual and physical abuse, I've finally found out what I deserve. Working for a company with a zero-tolerance policy in a male-dominated industry has done that. I'm more confident than I have ever been.

Roxy's company has earned her loyalty.

> I know I am hard working and reliable and they let me know that. At my performance review, my score always exceeds the top mark. The company makes sure the staff has full health benefits as well as subsidization for post-secondary and adult education classes.

We have regular staff appreciation events—pizza days and steak lunches catered from the Ranchman's. We have a Christmas party where you pay and when you show up you get your money back. There's a company baseball and curling team and an annual golf tournament. The company supports the Terry Fox Run for Cancer Research as well as several community projects. After Hurricane Katrina hit New Orleans, our head office started a donation fund for the victims. When a family member of mine was diagnosed with cancer, they gave me time off with no questions asked. Just as the company values me and the world I live in, I have also learned to value myself.

### Herstory Take-Aways:

- If working in the trades, be prepared to work physically hard. Once you prove you're capable, you'll be okay.
- Don't kill yourself trying to keep up physically with *the boys*.
- Don't let men's comments intimidate you.
- Seek to work for respectful and inclusive organizations.

### The Rest of Herstory:

ROXY ANDERSON'S employer, a large plumbing wholesaler, recently promoted her to dispatcher. She has earned the respect of clients and employees alike. As she says, "I have a lot more responsibility and hearing how happy my drivers (male and female) are is a nice payback." On her off-hours, she enjoys spending time with her grandchildren, beagle, cat, extended family and friends. Her next goal is to learn how to swim.

## 7. Moral Dilemma

THE Virtues Project presents a framework for educators, families and communities to encourage good character and respectful behavior in children. Author, Linda Popov, writes, "While values are culture specific, virtues are universally valued by all cultures." The program presents ways to instill basic virtues such as care, forgiveness, humility, justice and kindness. Moral dilemmas arise when two virtues or moral positions collide. For example, what do you do if your colleague has poor body odor? Do you approach the subject with kindness, honesty or some combination of both?

Moral dilemmas provide the premise of one of my favorite group games, *Scruples*. Cards present a predicament such as, "You see a co-worker steal an armful of office supplies. Do you report the incident to management?" Answer options include *yes, no* or *it depends*. The game requires you to back up your position based on your values. Moral dilemmas are circumstances in which no clear or morally correct answer or action is evident. Your own integrity takes on a crucial role.

*Let them know, "This may work for you but it definitely doesn't work for me."*

A survey respondent and project manager described her most challenging work experience as, "being let go for reporting an ethics violation on the company's ethics hotline." Woe! Perhaps the firing was a blessing. Otherwise, I imagine, she would have been caught in a moral dilemma and felt out of integrity sitting at her desk. Most employees want to feel proud of their work and their organizations. It's becoming common for young job interviewees to ask companies about their position and policies with respect to environmental or global concerns.

In the mid-1990s, DONNA KENNEDY-GLANS was vice-president of an international company when the company decided to invest in Nigeria. At that time, Nigeria was in social unrest, at the bottom of Transparency International's index with political discussions afoot to have it removed from the Commonwealth. Donna's reaction was a blast of questions.

> Aren't you aware that Nigeria is a pariah state; that corruption is pervasive; that Sani Abacha is an evil dictator; that local communities are bearing the full weight of investment (oil spills, contaminated water, gas flares) yet receiving little or no allocation of the benefits of development?

Regardless of the moral dilemma, the corporation moved ahead. Donna describes the subsequent activity, "This necessitated that the company re-evaluate its boundaries, and re-assess its accountabilities. I'll forever be grateful to my corporate colleagues for their courage in allowing those conversations." Her company's position was to become part of the Nigerian solution, not the problem. Donna's team made numerous business trips to Nigeria to meet with citizens, local government and investors. They concluded they could make a positive difference in two fundamental ways—advocate for gas flaring reduction or elimination and confront corruption through dialogue and alliances. The situation in Nigeria did improve and Donna did not have to sacrifice her moral integrity. She believes, "The moment you give in to the idea that a woman can't function under certain circumstances, you set yourself up to be angry for the rest of your life."

Astonishingly, when she first started working at a law firm, Donna was encouraged to choose Family Law over Corporate and Commercial law. She was even told by some male lawyers, "Maybe you picked the wrong career." She didn't accept this sexually-biased message and became a key player in international affairs in over 30 countries from Canada to the Congo to Yemen.

Perhaps it was this kind of tenacity that sustained her in facing and dealing with the moral challenge in Nigeria.

Donna used many resilience strengthening strategies to protect herself from giving in to the negative components of the company's involvement in Nigeria. She focused on what was possible. She trusted in the goodwill of others without being naïve. She talked to friends, colleagues and a supportive partner while ultimately returning to her own values as guideposts. She practiced yoga, walked, took hikes, wrote and pondered her situation. She never lost confidence in herself. As she says, "That's resiliency!" She believes, "Whatever you are uniquely equipped to do, that is your role in life." Plus, she became an expert on integrity. She knows when she's out of alignment with her values. She advises:

> Don't get focused on a single incident so that you are unable to see the past or the future. Contextualize the situation. It's important to have perspective. The minute you see yourself either as a victim or a hero, you have buried yourself.

### Herstory Take-Aways:

- Act in integrity. Integrity is the complete alignment of your intentions, commitments, and actions.
- Integrity dilemmas are inevitable.
- Avoid judging situations, people, companies, communities and countries.
- There is always more than one solution to a problem. Discern with care what is possible.

### The Rest of Herstory:

DONNA KENNEDY-GLANS is the co-author of *Corporate Integrity: A Toolkit for Managing Beyond Compliance*. One of the most powerful statements in her book is, "To be effective, we need to bring our whole person to the task of being a Moral Compass." Donna is the founder of Bridges Social Development, an organization working in Yemen, the Middle East, North Africa and the Near East to help transition women in male dominated workplaces.

Further initiatives are planned for youth projects in India, Yemen and Aboriginal communities in Canada. For more information, visit <**www.canada bridges.com**>. In 2008, Donna was chosen by Global TV as a Woman of Vision. To learn more about this lawyer and businesswoman who has evolved into an humanitarian, author and speaker, visit <**www. integritybridges.com**>.

## 8. Business Betrayal

Betrayal and broken trust deeply hurt. It amazed me to witness the demise of three businesses founded by colleagues of mine—six psychologist acquaintances. Two by two, they began therapeutic practices and eventually felt betrayed by one another. They parted and no longer speak to each other. One has to wonder, "If professionals who are in the relationship and healing business can't keep their agreements and trust intact, what chance is there for the rest of us?"

*It takes two to make a successful partnership and only one to ruin it.*

A survey respondent and manager wrote about her upset of "being overlooked for promotion twice." Others wrote, "My boss stealing my ideas and passing them off as her own" and "Co-workers spreading rumors that are false." Ill will can stick in your throat and stomach for a long time.

Naturally, one of the most immediate reactions to betrayal is to ask, "Why me?" Other common reactions include feelings of anger, disgust at the violator's lack of integrity and fantasies of revenge. Typically, the more we trusted someone, the more we feel violated and emotionally distraught. Also, the bigger the betrayal, the less likely trust will ever be re-established.

Some people choose the route of the justice system seeking to right the wrong done to them. It doesn't matter whether we seek remuneration, retribution or revenge, letting go of resentment is never easy. Consider Barbara Thrasher's story.

Barbara Thrasher started her first company, a Merle Norman franchise, when she was 21 years old. Her first business grew to be one of the top ten Merle Norman distributors in the world. Many years, several businesses and a multitude of bruises in the school of hard-knocks later, she became a small business consultant with a national client base.

At one point in one of her company's growth, she took on a partner in order to help out the woman, who was going through a bad time. Then, it happened. Like an out-of-control nightmare, her business partner had company contracts signed over into her own name. Barbara was beset with a multitude of business challenges at the time and had to declare bankruptcy to save parts of the company. As Barbara describes it:

> She betrayed me so she could walk away with her own business. If you would have asked me, I would have literally staked my life on her integrity. It wasn't just the financial blow but the emotional blow that shattered all my belief in how I saw my world.

Forgiveness did not come easily. It took Barbara two years of soul searching and reading to get there and to accept that forgiveness is something we have to do over and over if we are to be healthy and whole ourselves.

Forgiveness leads to improved physical and mental health as well as better relationships. Some books Barbara recommends are *Forgiveness Is a Choice: A Step-By-Step Process for Resolving Anger and Restoring Hope* by Robert D. Enright; *A Little Book of Forgiveness: Challenges and Meditations for Anyone with Something to Forgive* by D. Patrick Miller; *Forgive and Forget: Healing the Hurts We Don't Deserve* by Lewis B. Smedes; *The Language of Letting Go* by Melody Beattie; *When Smart People Fail* by Carole Hyatt and Linda Gottlieb; and *Invisible Acts of Power* by Caroline Myss.

Barbara's research and inner examination culminated in an observation of her tendency to either *blame throw* or *blame own* her problems. It's easy to get into this finger-pointing posture with a culture that habitually seeks to find the person who made the mistake or caused the problem. Just ask a politician how the media treats a perceived error. In the past, there had been incidents when her former business partner had acted without integrity but Barbara had chosen to ignore her tendency. She had rationalized her ex-business partner's behavior and made excuses for her choices. Her research in betrayal and forgiveness described this tendency to seek explanations as part of the process of letting go.

She concluded:

> Don't try to make up excuses for them (the betrayers). Like most women who carve out careers, we're doers. We push around holes, patch the missing gaps, overlook words

spoken to hurt us and disregard actions that are meant to undo us. We massage to try to fix others. But the situation is what it is. Nothing we can do will fix it. Our only option is to fix ourselves.

During those two years of soul searching, Barbara was aware that her pain might burst out on others and shut some doors. She chose trusted people carefully. "I was careful to speak to people who could really be helpful; not people who were caught into thinking they had to take sides." She also had the task of learning to forgive herself for naïvely trusting. As she described it, "Finally, I realized I had a choice; to hate her forever and feel suspicious of everyone or forgive her and get on with my life." Barbara forgave and moved on. The universe supported her decision. "I have been rewarded a hundred fold with strong business relationships and people who have been unbelievably generous and kind."

Philosophically, Barbara now describes starting over again.

The faster you can forgive the other person and yourself and recover, the less of an issue it is. In business and in our personal lives, there are issues that need to be addressed and individuals (including ourselves) that need to be forgiven. I have gone from taking two years to get back on track after being betrayed, to being able to recover when it pops back into my mind within minutes. It is all in how I choose to let the other person affect me, even as I deal with the challenges that any betrayal brings in its wake.

### Herstory Take-Aways:

- Forgive others for their transgressions rather than walk and talk with bitterness.
- Forgive yourself for not being all, seeing all and knowing all.
- Decide on your time to move on.
- Believe "there is always enough."
- Remember, although it hurts and it is hard to start again, often better clients come and opportunities open when old doors close.

### The Rest of Herstory:

BARBARA THRASHER'S most recent business, Work-Life Resources Inc., which can be found at <**www.work-liferesources.com**>, is thriving. In the past four years, they have helped over 1,000 managers reduce their stress and reduce their workloads. She builds her sense of abundance by spending time with loving family and friends, meditates, practices yoga, gardens and walks in nature. In 2007, she was chosen by Global TV and YWCA as a Woman of Vision.

## 9. Spousal Betrayal

THE most sacred union of all takes a daily battering in divorce courts all over the world. Four survey recipients described their divorce as the most stressful personal experience that affected their work. Here are some facts about divorce rates:

- **American Statistics**: Fifty percent of first marriages, 67 percent of second and 74 percent of third marriages end in divorce, according to Jennifer Baker of the Forest Institute of Professional Psychology in Springfield, Missouri.
- **Canadian Statistics**: First marriages have about a 50 percent chance of ending in divorce—about 72 percent for second and about 85 percent for third marriages. Almost 75 percent of Canadian divorces are being initiated by women. *The Department of Justice, Child Support Initiative, Evaluation Report,* August 1997.

*"I would have been more successful if I had a wife like me."*

It is a well accepted rule-of-thumb in the therapeutic community that a minimum of two years is required to rebuild a life after the breakup of a marriage. My own observations of clients, friends and family support this time line. Rarely do two people part on mutual and friendly terms. Typically, women walk away—sometimes run away—with doubts about their self-worth, sanity and financial stability. This is usually coupled with concerns about their ability to cope with all the changes that they and their children now face. Sometimes, women quickly recover but more often they temporarily crumble. A Corporate Information Manager and survey respondent reported that her divorce and ensuing custody battle was the most difficult personal and professional time of her life. WOW-Empowered Debbie D. Johnson echoes her sentiments.

When I first met **DEBBIE JOHNSON**, she was crawling her way out of emotional and financial trauma. She was enrolled in the *Contemporary Woman* project, a 12-week program available to women on social assistance or unemployment insurance. As program facilitators, my colleagues and I provided emotional support, career guidance and strategies for personal development. Debbie needed all the support we could offer. She was separated with two young children, had no money and was emotionally unable to work.

Debbie had met her husband and future business partner at church. It felt like a match made in heaven—and it seemed so for the 12 years they were married, until the day she discovered that her husband was married to another woman. Debbie was the *senior wife*.

The business that the two were involved in necessitated him traveling between Canada and China where he married his second wife. After Debbie discovered his secret, he asked that they remain married and business partners. He said, "What's the big deal? I am a great husband and father when I am at home." It was a big deal! The marriage ended.

Debbie describes her dilemma:

> I was married to a bigamist. I was sole owner of a business in China that my husband and I worked in. When I found out about his other wife, he removed $200,000 of our inventory in Hong Kong and breached contracts for which I became liable. I was consequently threatened with legal action by international companies. He filled the credit cards and emptied the children's RESP account. He told me by phone that he needed to support his other family. He spent over $50,000 in Hong Kong hotel rooms while he lived in his own apartment there.
>
> Furthermore, I had personally guaranteed one of our business contracts and, as a result, lost everything of any value to bankruptcy. I was in serious trouble. I no longer had a home for my children nor had the ability to work because my blood pressure skyrocketed and I developed Idiopathic Glomerulonephritis (kidney disorder). I wanted to die. Every smell and sound from the day I found out still resonated in my mind. A friend brought over a carton of cigarettes and a case of alcohol and I stayed in my little room learning how to smoke and how to get drunk.

Her emotions were on a roller coaster with each bottom a bit lower than the last. Then Debbie realized she needed help. She asked a friend to come and babysit her for a couple of days while she searched for sanity.

> The brain does funny things and I thought I smelled, constantly putting deodorant and perfume on. After all, it must have been some fault of mine that he did this to me. I felt ugly and thrown in the trash.

She watched her neighbors move her beautiful and trendy home furnishings into the surrounding homes' basements for temporary storage. She could have moved in with her parents but, to stabilize her children's environment, she moved into a friend's unfinished basement until her name hit the top of the subsidized housing list. The distress caused her a loss of confidence, a never-ending well of tears and humiliation about accepting welfare at 40 years of age. Later, she would say to taxpayers, "Thank you for paying taxes or I wouldn't have survived."

Her rebound included letting go of unsupportive friends who spoke judgmentally with lines such as, "You're turning into one of those people...those welfare people who have messy backyards," or "What did you do to *him*?" She also knew she needed to pursue a new career path. "I would have been a doctor but I decided that my kids were still too young for me to intern." After graduating from the *Contemporary Woman* project, Debbie chose to study law. She researched which undergraduate studies had the highest percentage of acceptance into law school and started her undergraduate degree. She finished it in four years, applied to law school and began to study law.

One of Debbie's most strengthening strategies was editing and empowering her mental thoughts. She began to *sweet-talk* herself with, "I'm nice. I did something kind today. I'm a beautiful person. I went to school, looked after my kids and was up at 3:00 AM doing my homework. I still have gold in me." She began to mentally image herself as a tree.

> That tree was a big deal. As a tree, I thought, "I can't move and this is it!" That forced me to stop and think about breathing—to sit still and *just* breathe. If I couldn't change the situation, I'd take control over what I could.

Debbie strengthened herself from the inside out.

Debbie has one last thought for those who are reconstructing their life. "Start with baby steps. You are alive. Life will only get better."

*Herstory Take-Aways:*

- Know, if necessary, your life can be rebuilt.
- Tell the truth and live your truth.
- Cleanse your circle of people who speak judgmentally and plant seeds of self-doubt.
- Use your fine mind to solve problems.
- Consciously edit what you think and say to yourself and others.

### *The Rest of Herstory:*

DEBBIE D. JOHNSON became an award-winning student and distinguished Bachelor of Arts and Bachelor of Laws graduate from The University of Calgary. She bought her family a house, is financing her children's university education and works at a law firm where women empower one another and are free to say, "No, I don't agree."

## 10. Caregiver Demands

MY mother told to me that raising children required a tremedous amount of energy and it's best to raise them when you are younger. I believed her and ended up with three children before I was 31. But then there were some days I would mutter, "Lies mothers tell us! I wish I had waited until I was older, calmer and wiser." Regardless of the age of the parents, children require food, shelter, clothing, time, routine, guidance and lots of love. How do parents fit children's needs in when they also have career demands? Some people have co-operative and supportive partners but many wish for that perfect spouse who will clean up the dishes, vacuum the house and prepare a gourmet meal. Some parents are able to negotiate part-time employment while more wish for it.

*How did we ever come to believe we could do it all alone?*

Almost all employed mothers who are divorced, separated, or cohabiting say the same thing. Caregiving has traditionally been entrusted to women, and still is. As noted with Linda's Bradburn's story about guilt, 28 survey respondents reported that their biggest Woes were home and family demands while an additional 13 said that the pull between home and workplace was their most significant challenge.

### Solo Mom Isolation

Kelly, our daughter, is a single-parent mom to our three grandchildren. Our son, Benjamin, has recently married Amy, a single parent with an eight-year-old. Kelly and Amy have had years of being the only one available when a child cried in the night. Upon reflection, I feel privileged to have a long-term marriage that provided a back-up mind, body and two extra hands. Where are the fathers? In Canada, one year after separation or divorce, 50 percent of the children never see their fathers again. Here are some other figures from Statistics Canada:

- 550,000 — The estimated number of single-parent families headed by women in Canada in 2004.
- $27,700 — The after-tax income of lone-parent families headed by women in 2004.

Some days, I think we should salute solo moms for their persistence in raising their children. Often, with minimal free time and minimum income, little reserve is left for emergencies. Definitely, the rest of us look on asking, "How does she do it?" Here's Leane's story.

For several years, LEANE RILEY had been a single mom raising two little girls while working full-time as a company clerk. One evening, she returned home to discover that one of her daughters had been sexually assaulted. Leane immediately contacted authorities and her daughter received the medical and psychological attention she needed. But Leane was overcome with guilt and had no idea who to turn to for support. The next morning, she revealed to her manager that her daughter had been sexually assaulted. She intended to present *just the facts* but, as she related the story, tears began to flow. Leane recalled, "I knew I didn't have to tell her but I thought that I would get some understanding and support." While relaying the nightmare, her manager sat leg up on knee with crossed arms like a chilly and locked freezer. The manager's voice, posture and facial expression remained frozen—no sympathy or compassion. Her only words were, "What is your plan for work?" Leane responded, "I don't know."

Amazingly enough, Leane worked every day that week. On Friday, while struggling to focus, she had a revelation. She remembered a woman in her department who had incurred an injury but had not reported it and, therefore, had not received compensation. Leane had encouraged her to use the company's disability plan. At that moment, Leane realized that she needed to take her own advice and use the company's disability plan to take care of herself and her daughter. She contacted her doctor and arranged for a three-week leave. The manager contacted Leane once to ask about a file but never to inquire how she was. When Leane returned to work after her leave, her manager promptly took her into another office and handed her a letter stating that her position had been collapsed. She accepted the severance package and never returned.

Leane describes how she coped:

> When my job was terminated, I was immediately cut off from access to the company's compensation plan. Instead, I developed my own support network. The social worker at the Children's Hospital provided valuable information—books to read and community services to access. I began intense counseling and asked whoever was available for help with the girls when I had a counseling session or doctor's appointment. During this time, it was important that the girls were with someone they knew and someone they could trust. It was equally important for me to know that when I wasn't there, they were safe. One friend, in particular, was there at the drop of a hat. She provided a place to vent and a safe place to cry. I also looked to my daughter to reinforce my courage. I realized that, more than ever, routine and structure were important for both my girls. It was also important for me. I was determined not to let them or me down.

### Herstory Take-Aways:

- Care for yourself and your children first.
- Realize that no one is indispensable in the workplace.
- Choose how personal you make your work experience.
- Look for the best choice for you and your family to acquire a paycheck.

### The Rest of Herstory:

With part-time employment, LEANE RILEY now lives with her pre-teen girls and a supportive partner. Leane describes her present manager as someone who encourages her to take credit for her contributions to the company. Her manager also acknowledges the importance of family. Leane says, "He respects people, their family and their kids. His value of *family first* aligns with mine." See Leane's *Tips for Single Moms* on page 175.

### The Challenges for All Caregivers

A survey conducted by Canada's Vanier Institute of the Family found that 90 percent of Canadians polled believe that (in two-parent families) one parent should stay home to care for the children. They also found that 90 percent of mothers who are married and employed would work part-time if they could afford to, as would 84 percent of fathers. A US national survey by Public Agenda, a non-profit policy organization, reported that 70 percent of parents with children five and under say one parent at home is the best arrangement.

When we factor in other challenges—caring for children with disabilities or handicaps or elderly parents who require assistance—we compound the demands on our time and energy.

As an advocate of caregivers, BEVERLEY SMITH keeps tabs on these kinds of statistics and stories. Although her primary job is as a full-time substitute teacher, Beverley is best known for her work as a researcher and writer advocating for the recognition and valuing of unpaid caring for children, caring for those with disabilities and handicaps and caring for the elderly and the dying. She is so passionate about her work that she has taken on the Canadian government. She recognizes that government already supports paid versions of care through services such as childcare and homecare.

Unlike many who use outside interests to bring perspective to their workplace challenges, Beverley teaches to sustain her activism. She says:

> I have found that anyone with long-term commitments to a cause has to have leisure activities or paid work that is compelling to distract and refresh them. I find that working with school kids (Kindergarten to Grade 12) cheers me up and certainly gives me lots more material for why I care so much about these issues.

When Beverley made a complaint to the Canadian Human Rights Commission about tax and pension law discrimination against those who do unpaid care work, she received nearly no response. Years later, through *access to information* legislation, she discovered a memo between two civil servants. It referred to her work, "If you like, we can discuss trying to *kill* this more completely." Beverley made a copy of this memo, framed it and mounted it in her bedroom to spur her on. For 22 years, Beverley has petitioned government, organized rallies, met with Members of Parliament and made presentations to committees of government. She filed a complaint with the United

Nations that Canada's tax, pension and childcare laws discriminate against some care options. The Canadian government wrote a "scathing criticism of my argument, and tried to downplay the whole thing to the press."

Holding down full-time employment while taking on the country's government is no small task and has had repeated setbacks. Beverley not only advocates for the importance of (typically women's) unpaid work but also lives her talk. In addition to her teaching as a balancing force, her family and leisure activities sustain her.

Typical of the women interviewees of this book, Beverley makes deliberate efforts to attend to her physical, mental, social and spiritual needs. Family conversations, activities with her grandchildren and time spent walking her dogs keep her balanced and healthy.

## Herstory Take-Aways:

- Recognize that caregiving is demanding and should be better valued in our culture.
- Create your own *work-family balance* formula.
- Acknowledge that the challenge of *work-family balance* is still primarily a women's issue.
- Choose supports that work for you—child care, day home, nanny, friends, relatives, dad or mom at home, dad or mom off-shifting each other.
- Seek the best work situation for you and your family—part-time employment, a home-based office, telecommuting or other flexible arrangements.

## The Rest of Herstory:

BEVERLEY SMITH'S petition to the United Nations was supported by numerous international organizations. Though Canada officially denied her claims, the UN Working group concluded there was an international trend of an absence of women in decision-making, there were legal systems discriminating in the complainant countries, and there was a high incidence of women and children in poverty. Beverley was named 1999 Calgarian of the Year by *Business in Calgary* magazine and received the Queen's Golden Jubilee Medal. To subscribe to Beverley's *Anchors Away* e-newsletter with research on caregiving, contact her at <**bevgsmith@alumni.ucalgary.ca**>.

# IV

# Strengthening Your Resilience

Choose Your
WOW Strategies

W **OW STRATEGIES** describe resilience-strengthening behaviors that can be practiced by anyone. They are based on information gleaned from counseling and consulting, positive psychology and resilience research, plus responses from interviewees and audience surveys. Consider the information and processes in the following section as a reservoir of resources available for you to access when *the going gets tough*. You can decide when, where and with whom they best fit. They will help you answer the question, "What can I do?"

## Reservoir of WOW Strategies

Accept ambiguity and contradictions

Accept that change happens

Acknowledge and Demonstrate Your Strengths – IV:2, p. 151

Align with Integrity – I:2 p. 91

Apologize and make amends

Ask questions

Attend to Your Body – II:7. p. 122

Be a Dear with Two Ears: Listen – III:1, p. 126

Be Laid Off Without Laying Down – IV:6, p. 160

Be a Brazen Gal: Self Promote – V:2, p. 167

Breathe and Get Grounded – III:3, p. 134

Champion Change –IV:1, p. 150

Choose *Your* Best Life Rhythm – I:6, p. 98

Create Your Village – V:5, p. 174

Declare your values

Delegate

Demonstrate Courage – IV:4, p. 156

Develop empathy

Ease Conflict – III:4, p. 137

Eat nutritious foods

Edit out negative self-talk

Embrace Your *Womanness* – I:4, p. 95

Establish Clear Boundaries – I:1, p. 87

Exercise regularly

Filter Criticism: Offer Feedback – III:6, p. 142

First, Care for the Mother – I:5, p. 97

Foster supportive relationships

Get a Little Help from Your Friends – V:3, p. 169

Get Familiar with Protective Laws – I:7, p. 102

Give Up Your Grudge – V:6, p. 176

Give and Receive Acknowledgement – V:1, p. 165

Give and receive helpful feedback

Go Back to School, *Maybe* – IV:5, p. 158

Have a *Good* Cry – III:5, p. 117

Honor Your Feelings – II:3, p. 112

Initiate your own joy and pleasure

Keep Your *Humanness* – I:3, p. 93

Learn from set-backs and challenges

Lighten Up! – II:6, p. 120

*Make Up Your Mind*, Decide – IV:3, p. 154

Manage Management – III:7, p. 145

Move Out of Painful Feelings – III:4, p. 115

Muster courage

Name and own your part of the problem

Negotiate

Nurture a Supportive Love Relationship – V:4, p. 172

Plan for Resolution – III:5, p. 139

Pray or meditate

Put Pollyanna to Shame: Think Optimistically – II:1, p. 105

Quit or Resign – IV:7, p. 161

Rest and sleep well

Say *yes* and *no*

Seek an Inclusive and Respectful Workplace – V:7, p. 179

Speak Up: Assert or You'll Blurt – III:2, p. 129

Sweet-Talk to Yourself – II:2, p. 109

Trust yourself

Uphold human rights

# I
## Protect Your Inner WOW Woman

*Use your inner wisdom to shield yourself from the outside voices of judgment, criticism and diminishment.*

- Establish Clear Boundaries
- Align with Integrity
- Keep Your *Humanness*
- Embrace Your *Womanness*
- First, Care for the Mother
- Choose *Your* Best Life Rhythm
- Get Familiar with Protective Laws

## 1. Establish Clear Boundaries

Pᴇʀꜱᴏɴᴀʟ boundaries provide an effective WOW strategy to handle many different external woes or adversities. Among survey respondents who would have benefited from stronger boundaries was an outreach worker who wrote, "I wish I'd stood up to her," and the office receptionist who wrote, "I should have stood up for myself months sooner," and the nurse who wrote, "I didn't make the world a better place by running away." Think of personal boundaries as similar to survey lines between neighboring properties. The line says, "My property begins and ends here." Some people mark their boundaries with a brick wall—hard, no entry gate and gives no sense of who or what is on the other side. Some people have boundaries similar to a fallen down fence—leaving the rest of us questioning whether we're welcome to enter or not. Some people appear to have no boundaries until they yell at us for crossing an undefined line. Just as *good fences make good neighbors*, healthy boundaries make healthy relationships.

*"It's not good for me to say, Yes."*

Anne Katherine wrote in *Boundaries: Where You End and I Begin*, "With good boundaries, we can have the wonderful assurance that comes from knowing we can and will protect ourselves from the ignorance, meanness or thoughtlessness of others." We have physical, verbal, emotional, relationship, spiritual and sexual boundaries. To maintain our boundaries we need to choose wisely to what we say *yes, no* or *it depends*. Basically, clear boundaries help us protect our value system. Many values have to do with our personal story or history. Values are those qualities, people, behaviors and things we hold as important or worthy. We can identify our values by noting how we invest our time, money and energy.

On the following chart, note your five most important values. Consider which values you invest the most:

- Money
- Time seeking
- Time developing
- Energy or focus

## Values Chart

| | | | | |
|---|---|---|---|---|
| acceptance | achievement | adventure | acknowledgement | animals |
| appreciation | art | balance | beauty | belonging |
| caring | challenge | change | children | comfort |
| compassion | competition | commitment | communication | control |
| cooperation | creativity | courage | dignity | discipline |
| diversity | economic security | education | emotional maturity | equality |
| enthusiasm | ethics | excellence | fame | faith |
| family | feelings | financial security | freedom | friendship |
| fun | generosity | gentleness | harmony | health |
| helping others | home | human rights | humor | humility |
| idealism | influence | integrity | intuition | joy |
| justice | kindness | law and order | listening | logic |
| loyalty | love | manners | modesty | money |
| music | mystery | native culture | native traditions | nature |
| nurturing | orderliness | passion | patience | peace |
| personal development | play | pleasure | power | prayer |
| prestige | privacy | recognition | reliability | resilience |
| respect | responsibility | reverence | risk taking | sacredness |
| seniors | sensitivity | sensuality | sex | sharing |
| silence | spirituality | sports & fitness | solitude | success |
| synergy | teamwork | tenderness | thinking | tolerance |
| touch | travel | truth | trustworthiness | unity |
| vision | winning | wisdom | other? | |

When we clarify our values, intentions and boundaries our messages become clear and less emotionally driven. We will declare what is acceptable and unacceptable to us in a calm and non-judgmental manner. The only person over whom we have power is ourselves. To put our personal power into action we can declare what we will and will not do and then *follow through*.

Here is how to create a **3-Point Boundary Declaration** using your values:

- **VALUE:** "Speaking respectfully is important to me."
- **FEELING:** "I feel hurt."
- **RESULT** (state what action *you* will take)

  – **Positive:** "*If you choose* to speak respectfully, *I will* stay."
  – **Negative:** "*If you choose* to swear at me, *I will* leave."

It's up to you to follow through on your end of the boundary declaration. In the above example you maintain your boundary by either staying or leaving.

### Moral Dilemmas

Sometimes values conflict with one another. Career women often value the stimulation and intellectual challenge of employment while feeling guilty about leaving their children in alternate care. There is no right or wrong. As discussed in the next section, remaining in integrity when in a moral dilemma requires effort and soul searching.

### The No Dilemma

You may be like many women who say *yes* when they want to say *no*. We were sold a bill of goods that it wasn't nice to say no. The result can include a loss of self-respect, over extending ourselves, becoming ill or blowing up at others with resentful feelings.

Oprah Winfrey refers to *The Disease to Please*. As little girls, many of us were trained in the habit of pleasing grown ups so we might receive needed attention and love. We worked to *make them* feel happy so they would say or do something to *make us* happy. We worked to *make them* feel appreciated so they would say or do something to *make us* feel appreciated. We worked to *make them* feel proud of us so they would say or do something to *make us* feel proud.

That becomes a lot of others *making us*. This is an example of *external locus of control* or dependence on others for our care and satisfaction. As children, it is true that we have little control and power. We did depend on our caregivers. But, at some

### Ten Tips for Saying *No*

*"No is the world's most powerful stress management word."*

1. Ensure that you give *no*, *yes* and *it depends* consideration.
2. Give yourself time to consider the request by saying, "I'd like to think about it."
3. Repeat the request before saying, "Thank you for asking but *no*."
4. Offer an alternative with, "*No*, but what I will do is…"
5. Suggest that someone else is better suited for the task.
6. When appropriate, explain why you are saying *no*. "I'm saying *no* because…"
7. State the conditions that will help you meet a request. "After I finish this assignment I will do it."
8. Explain what is not good for your group, team or company. "The most effective use of my time is…"
9. Show you care. "I hear you are in a bind and I wish I could do more but…"
10. Ensure you say *no* in an appropriate manner and not in violation of company policies or procedures.

point, we benefit by declaring our adulthood, making decisions that reflect our matured values and sticking to them.

In some ways, one of the developmental tasks of becoming an adult is to act as our own caregiver, to be our own loving and guiding parent. One of the hardest and necessary parental jobs is saying *no*. If saying *no* is a challenge for you, begin to have an internal dialogue that is lovingly supportive and yet self-controlling. "I value my time. I will decide if and when I will give it away."

Hearing *no* for children and adults can be disappointing. After all, don't we make a request when we believe someone can give us what we need or want? We can easily interpret the word as rejection. Hence, for women who classically care deeply about relationships, the word is hard to say. One day, when I was feeling overwhelmed by our three children, I called my friend, Mabel, to arrange some relief. She kindly and politely responded by saying, "I'd like to but today it's not good for me to say *yes*." I was blown away! At first I felt disappointed. But, in the second breath, I felt connected to her. I admired her self-care. If I pushed her to meet my request, I would be giving the message,

"I don't care what's good for you." I too began to say, "It's not good for me to say *yes*." Feel free to use that little strategy if you struggle with *no*.

Acknowledge when you feel proud of yourself. Of course it's wonderful to receive care, appreciation and encouragement from others. Enjoy it while not relying on the outside to *feed* you. Choose to absolutely live your own truth and nurture your own self-respect. Learn to say *yes* and *no* to reflect who you are. You will earn your own respect, if not that of your co-workers and family.

## 2. Align with Integrity

THE Merriam-Webster dictionary defines *integrity* as "firm adherence to a code of especially moral or artistic values or incorruptibility." In 2002, *Time* magazine's "People of the Year" were three women-of-integrity or, as the media headlines screamed, *whistle-blowers*. Coleen Rowley, an agent at the Federal Bureau of Investigation criticized the FBI for ignoring evidence of terrorist plans before the September 11 attacks. Both Sherron Watkins of *Enron* and Cynthia Cooper of *WorldCom* reported fraudulent activity within their respective companies. These women just couldn't go to sleep at night without doing something that was in alignment with their values. They all risked—both personally and professionally—the chagrin of colleagues and management by their actions. For each of them, the greater risk was in not acting and thereby losing integrity.

*Walk away feeling true to yourself.*

I haven't been featured on the cover of *Time* magazine but, about ten years ago, I wrote a letter of resignation along with 12 recommendations which addressed 12 moral dilemmas that drove me out of the organization. A copy was forwarded to both the Director and the Board of Directors. I walked away believing I had done my part in naming what was unjust. My popularity within that agency plummeted to the bottom but I survived. I thrived.

In her book, *Corporate Integrity*, Donna Kennedy-Glans defines integrity as "the complete alignment of your intentions, commitments and actions." She also offers an illuminating question to help make a decision, "Will my children and grandchildren appreciate my decision?" In this context, acts of integrity can be as significant as proceeding with care when contemplating doing business in a country known for human rights violations or as small as reducing, reusing and recycling products. In 1932, Herbert J. Taylor, who later became Rotarian International President, developed four simple questions as ethical guide posts. Before speaking or taking action, use **The 4-Way Test**:

1. Is it the truth?
2. Is it fair to all concerned?
3. Will it build goodwill and better friendships?
4. Will it be beneficial to all concerned?

Anita Roddick, creator of *The Body Shop*, shook the business world with her unorthodox practices. She made her company's message clear through this line, "There are three billion women in the world and only eight that look like supermodels." Not only did she challenge stereotypes of women's beauty but involved herself in activism and campaigning for environmental and social issues. She gave her staff time off to volunteer and once said, "...good business is also about putting forward solutions, not just opposing destructive practices or human rights abuses."

## Ten Tips for Detecting Out-of-Integrity

*"Oh! My gosh! What was I thinking?"*

1. You gave in to peer pressure.
2. You spoke or acted with poor intentions driven by urges of greed, pride, envy, revenge or deception.
3. You had disturbing flashbacks and nightmares of what you said or did.
4. You stood by or hid when harm occurred to yourself, others or the environment.
5. You felt guilt or regret.
6. You felt a sickness or sinking in your stomach.
7. You noticed critical self-talk yelling at you internally.
8. You received little or no support from those you trusted for wisdom, compassion and thoughtful discernment.
9. You were glad that children or those you respect were not present.
10. You concluded you could *save yourself* by making amends.

## 3. Keep Your *Humanness*

Hey there! Don't let your work define who you are. Ask someone what they do and you will often hear a title like *office administrator, teacher* or *engineer.* You are not your roles, thoughts, feelings, beliefs or work. These aspects of your life are all chosen by *you.* Identifying your self *only* through your work can become problematic. It represents a part of your life, not your whole. Careers allow us to show off our abilities. In self-esteem terms, we want to believe, "I am capable *and* I am lovable." A nurse reported in the survey, "Work is not that important in the big scheme of things." She's got it!

*Human needs include time for fun, sun and just being.*

In a culture that values people based on their accomplishments, we can easily avoid taking time and space to accept, let alone love, ourselves as is—perhaps lounging on the couch. That's what Gloria Steinem, a very successful and leading feminist, shared in her book, *Moving Beyond Words.* It took her years to figure out what was missing from her life. She wrote:

> The need for supporting core self-esteem doesn't end in childhood. Adults still need unconditional love from family, friends, life partners, animals, and perhaps even an all-forgiving deity. "No matter how the world may judge you, I love you for yourself."

We see unconditional love demonstrated in the care of a newborn baby as her parents awake night after night. It's the offer of shelter to a homeless person. It's the tail wagging on your dog. Our dog provided no household help, required regular walks, was fed and loved for *just being.* Sure, she was reprimanded for her *accidents*, but her unique lovableness was never questioned. Regrettably, many people are not given the same message of irreplaceable value.

To love yourself unconditionally means to treasure yourself merely because you exist. Think "existential." "Woo-woo," as my friend Jannette says. We've moved into a psychological and spiritual realm. Bear with me. The basic premise is that all beings are lovable and valuable. Yes, even those who break the law. I've written about that in my book, *Love Her As She Is.* Loving *as is* provides the underpinning concept. It separates the *doer* from the *deed*; the *being* from the *act.*

## Ten Tips to Avoid Workaholism

*"I reclaim my time and life."*

1. Prepare a daily To Do list including one column for business and one for personal. If later you think of another To Do and it's not urgent, save it for the next day.
2. Exercise each morning so that self-care is taken care of before work begins.
3. Don't be the last person to leave the office at night.
4. Delegate.
5. Avoid taking on responsibilities that don't belong to you. Say *"No!"*
6. Take a lunch break every day. If it can't be an hour, take a half hour.
7. If you *have to* work on the weekend, pick one day. Never work both days.
8. Find someone emotionally with whom you can verbalize your concerns about workaholism. Accept advice and put it into action!
9. If you work from a home office, avoid working into the night by making plans to read a book (non-work related) or go see a movie.
10. Forecast for the future. Set long-term goals with achievement dates. If you tend to do projects immediately, cut larger and longer assignments into smaller pieces that fit into your normal schedule.

*Source*: SUZY WILKOFF

If you are not already embracing yourself for simply being human in woman form, below are some self-affirming statements. Be gentle with yourself and don't force these beliefs. Dr. Al Siebert, author of *The Resiliency Advantage* and *The Survivor Personality*, cautions against forced affirmations as they may trigger a reverse reaction. These gentle words can become demons if spoken from an internal and demanding gremlin. If you find it difficult to tell yourself, "I deserve love," you might start by telling yourself, "I want to believe:

- I deserve love.
- I am a good and loving person.
- I am okay just the way I am.
- My needs and wants are important.
- I am lovable at every age."

Find a self-affirming statement that best works for you. It will be the one that settles comfortably in your mind and body. Notice how you feel when you tell yourself this message. Repeat the message to yourself more than you imagine you need to hear it.

If you need a reminder to do this, just remember the story of the young man who asked the New York taxi driver, "How do you get to Carnegie Hall?" The taxi driver's response was, "Practice, practice, practice." If you want to arrive at an *internal hall* of your own wellbeing, "Practice, practice, practice."

## 4. Embrace Your *Womanness*

Most workplaces make demands of women to develop their masculine side in male-developed hierarchies. They are expected to think logically, set goals and participate in competitive situations. Deborah Tannen, a linguistics specialist and author of *You Just Don't Understand*, examined the differing conversational styles of men and women. Here are some of her conclusions:

- Men prefer competition and attaining status in hierarchies by winning.
- Women prefer co-operation and support.
  Consider the typical games boys and girls play—jump rope or dolls for girls and bad guys/good guys for the boys. Recall men's put-down or sarcastic humor to maintain their one-up position while women giggle and accept a one-down position with "It was nothing," or self-deprecating lines such as, "Silly me."
- Men prefer independence.
- Women prefer relationships.
  Consider the many marriage-seeking women and the commitment-phobic men.
- Men prefer taking action, fixing or solving a problem.
- Women prefer giving and receiving emotional support.
  Consider how men use the phone to arrange to do something while women will talk for hours to indicate friendship and care.
- Men prefer facts and information.
- Women prefer feelings and intuition.
  Consider the guys at a party discussing the newest make of car while the women are commiserating over a bad hair day.
- Men prefer orders.
- Women prefer suggestions.

Consider men's directive of, "We're taking a break now," to women's hint-hint, "Let's take a break," or "Would you like to take a break?" desiring to be inclusive and hoping they will agree.

*What if the world celebrated the gifts and resources of both men and women?*

If these examples seem stereotypical, they are! Of course, there are exceptions to these generalizations. However, these socialization tendencies can help us understand and appreciate the other sex's preferences. Rather than blaming the other sex for our misunderstandings, we can begin to appreciate their differences. For example, in *Coping with the Male Ego*, authors Grymes and Stantan explain:

> Men are just beginning to learn how to compete with women. They have spent their lives competing with each other—learning to be aggressive, to take risks, to think and act logically, and to defend "the rules." Men know what to expect from other men. Competition is their relationships.

For example, men tend to view asking for help as acting vulnerable or being a loser. I witnessed this the day my husband tried to move a high-backed piano out of the house on his own. Why did Moses spend 40 years wandering in the desert? He didn't want to act like a woman and ask for directions. Asking for directions is a *one-down* position in which women tend to feel more comfortable. Alternatively, males typically respond well when asked for advice or help. He may even think, "Yes! I'm the winner!"

Men's use of language often reflects this tendency to be in competition. The more forceful and coarser the language, the more power they assume. A survey respondent working in the trades wrote of swearing by the male workers. "Men will be men and it doesn't mean that a woman will make them speak properly." Properly is politely, inclusively and sensitively; typically a woman's preference. This is not to say that foul language should necessarily be tolerated and is definitely not appropriate in professional circles.

Women and men have their own reality. To repeat myself, women are inclined to place emphasis, focus and priority on relationships and the welfare of others. I recall the nights when our children were sick and required comforting and the bed sheets changed. My husband slept through the night. How long does it take to listen to a crying

## Ten Tips for Strengthening the Yin and the Yang

*"She said, 'We need to talk.' He thought, 'Darn, I'll lose.'"*

1. If you feel offended, check out the other person's intention before responding.
2. Name and address sexism, discrimination and negative stereotyping.
3. Avoid acting too modestly. Show off your strengths, including those considered *feminine* or soft qualities.
4. Present your ideas in a confident manner.
5. Say, "I'm sorry," only when you need to make amends.
6. Use but don't over use self-deprecation. It may be interpreted as incapable.
7. Ask directly for advice and what you need or want. "Will you…?"
8. Adopt a good-natured attitude towards *friendly* competition. Don't tolerate mean-spirited competition.
9. Protect your emotions. Take them to those who can calmly witness them.
10. Celebrate your own and others feminine and masculine qualities.

friend? A man may say, "Five minutes should do it." Most women believe, "As long as she needs me to listen." Consequently, clock time and women time differ.

Differences between men's and women's preferences will remain for at least another generation or two. Yet, it's time to find ways to bridge the gap, to move towards the integration of the masculine and feminine qualities in us all.

## 5. First, Care for the Mother

You now have the most important job a woman will ever do," my mother told me after I gave birth. It's important for us to embrace the traditional feminine role of caregiver as a way to demonstrate our strengths and capabilities. A 2006 report from salary.com excited many of us interested in the world of moms. The grand conclusion was that mothers (typically with 2 children) would earn $131,471 US or $163,855 CDN a year if paid for the services rendered to their families. Regrettably, we can easily lose ourselves and forget to care for ourselves in the middle of doing these services. We can become over-whelmed, see few options and forget the answer to the question, "Who am I?"

> *Sometimes our distorted definition of "mother" is "no time, space or care for me."*

Some of us have been called *The Hurried Woman*, the *PMS Mom from H*…and told by our teenagers to "chill out." A research finding from Dalhousie University in Nova Scotia concludes that distress is taking its toll on Canadian women, especially mothers. The researcher, Shelley Phipps, was quoted as saying, "Over half…51.2 percent of women aged 25 to 54 with full-time paid employment felt constantly under stress in comparison with 41.6 percent of men." And this figure continues to increase. Add children and the fact that mothers still accept the majority of household responsibility and what do you get?—an out-of-functioning, often ill, woman—especially if she has negative perceptions of these demands.

The Canadian Stress Institute's research also supports these findings. Take the following quiz (see opposite) to help you with some proactive and protective steps.

## 6. Choose *Your* Best Life Rhythm

While 28 survey respondents identified their biggest challenge as care-giving demands, another 13 specifically described their major Woe or challenge with the term *balance*. One worker wrote, "Keeping balance between work and play," while a single parent reported,

> *Give up looking for balance. Ride life's teeter-totter ups and downs as gracefully as possible.*

"Balancing working and raising my six kids alone." Some call it *work-life balance*, others *work-family balance* or *work-home balance*. First, let's eliminate the phrase *work-life* because surely *work* is part of life and a significant part of it, for that matter. Secondly, *balance* may not be possible. The demands of work and family are more like a teeter-totter or a roller coaster where balance comes in some moments. Perhaps the best we can do is aim to maintain some kind of internal stability in the middle of the storm.

Beverley Smith, the Canadian caregiver advocate, believes the problem lies partly in the question. She views both employment and family responsibilities as *work*. It is genuine *work* to listen to a troubled teen, to make a family meal, to care for your senior parents or to get up several times at night with a newborn.

## Out of the Mommy Stress Bucket

Answer *Yes* or *No* to the following:

|  | Yes | No |
|---|---|---|
| 1. Are you free of anxiety, mood swings, tension headaches, fatigue, frequent colds, flu or insomnia? | ☐ | ☐ |
| 2. Are you free of the *Super Mom* or *Perfect Mom* trap and think of yourself as a *Good Enough Mom*? | ☐ | ☐ |
| 3. Are you available to your children in a supportive, relaxed, sometimes playful and loving manner? | ☐ | ☐ |
| 4. Do you delegate some household tasks to your partner and children? | ☐ | ☐ |
| 5. Do you have an attitude of "I appreciate an improvement" rather than insisting on tasks being accomplished to your standards? | ☐ | ☐ |
| 6. Do you hold family meetings where you enlist team participation of family members? | ☐ | ☐ |
| 7. Are you free of guilt when you see unhappy family members knowing that the only person you have control over is yourself? | ☐ | ☐ |
| 8. Do you say *no* to activities that needlessly take you away from personal, couple or family time? | ☐ | ☐ |
| 9. Are you aware that one of the biggest gifts you can give your family is your own wellbeing as a healthy and assertive woman who both gives and receives? | ☐ | ☐ |
| 10. Do you take daily time to rejuvenate yourself so that you can be present to your family mentally, physically, emotionally and spiritually? | ☐ | ☐ |

**Note**: The more questions to which you answered *yes*, the better you are taking care of yourself first. If your score is low, start to take the actions recommended in the above ten points. Raise your score until you believe you are of one of the best *good enough moms* on the block.

Often caregiving jobs are those for which we *did not apply*. Beverley notes, "We are all one phone call in the night from being caregivers." Since for some people care of the family *is* their career, perhaps women need to discuss the demands of paid work and unpaid work in the home and community.

Look at all your decisions holistically, including activities that nourish you physically, mentally, emotionally, socially, creatively and spiritually. How about experimenting with backing off on a task or two to make time and space for some self-rejuvenation? If you can financially afford to do so, pay for tasks that are a drag on you. If you can't afford that option, consider delegating tasks. "Delegate!?" you may ask.

Bear with me. I detect a groan and hear, "He (she, they) won't do it like I want. I have standards, you know." This is a very effective strategy for scaring away willing supporters. When moms are over-responsible, they rob other family members of demonstrating their capabilities. Parents do their children no favor by doing for them what children can do for themselves. Sometimes, as women, *our need to be needed* overshadows our need to have rest, relaxation, recreation and down time. Fortunately, you can change your belief to a sane position of, "I appreciate your cooperation and it doesn't have to be done perfectly."

Families in which support, cooperation and fairness are exercised have less conflict and illness. They put into action valuing their family relationships and teamwork. Please don't risk your health and your main support relationships over clean dirt, otherwise known as dust.

Another block to gaining family cooperation is using nagging and whining instead of invitation and negotiation. Nagging can be replaced by WOW strategies of creating clear boundaries, assertiveness and easing conflict. In addition, you could hold a Family Meeting. Not only do family meetings provide an opportunity to share the household load, they create a cooperative framework for sharing feelings and ideas, for supporting wishes and goals, for problem solving, for making future family plans and for increasing the pleasure, harmony and fun in the family home. For those involved in the care of aging parents, family meetings involving adult siblings can be an effective means to share the care.

# Family Meetings

*"We have a plan!"*

### Suggested Guideline:

1. Meet on a regular basis, at a specific time, for a specific length of time. After Sunday Dinner works for many families.
2. Utilize active listening and *"I"* messages to encourage clear communication.
3. Use the meetings to solve problems and to plan fun family events and outings.
4. Decide whether you want to keep minutes of your meetings. An adult might chair the meeting while a child might keep minutes. Trade responsibilities as the children learn notetaking and chairing skills.
5. Make clear commitments to one another. State either *I will* or *I won't*.
6. Expect minimal involvement from family members five years of age and under.

### Suggested Format:

1. **Share appreciations** from the previous week. *Example*: "Thank you, Dad, for fixing my bicycle." "Thank you, Johnny, for keeping your agreement to stay out of your sister's room."
2. **Evaluation of solutions** used in the previous week. *Example*: "We kept paper, toys and stuff off the stair steps all week and I think we have kept our family safer. I would like to recommend that we keep up this new habit."
3. **Problems identified (complaints) of the week**. Each person is allowed to identify one problem they want solved. They take *ownership* that it is their problem. *Example*: "I have a problem. I am not getting enough sleep. After everyone else is in bed, I do kitchen clean up, pack school lunches, tidy the house and do the laundry."
4. **Make a request.** *Example*: "I want to do less of the household tasks and for you to do more."
5. **Brainstorm optional solutions.** *Example*: "I could tidy up after meals. I could get a meal once a week. We could do our own laundry. We kids could make our own lunches. We could all clean the house together on Saturdays."
6. **Agree on your solution or solutions**. *Example*: "Do we all agree that the children will make their own lunches and we will clean the house together Saturday mornings?"
7. **End with a family game, activity or snacking treat.**

## 7. Get Familiar with Protective Laws

WOMEN before us risked slander and sometimes death so we might benefit from protective laws. It's a shame that we do not use them as they were intended. Regretably, discrimination and harassment continues in our workplaces, organizations and communities. When I was a career counselor assisting those on unemployment insurance to prepare and interview for jobs, I worked with a man the staff secretly called *Dinosaur Guy*. He treated me differently than he did the male professionals, referring to me as *The Blonde Dame*. Other derogatory terms for women included *Ditz Sticks* and *Peanut Brains*. No matter the gentle persuasion, the pleas, the confrontations about his demeaning and objectionable language, he just didn't clue in to his offensiveness. Countless women I have counseled have told me similar or more disturbing stories.

> *It's a shame not to use protective laws as they were intended.*

Behaviors that discriminate or harass can wear away self-esteem and confidence. Excerpts from the *Canadian Human Rights Act* will help clarify the line between wanting to be treated in a certain manner and a true right:

- For all purposes of this Act (*The Canadian Human Rights Act*), the prohibited grounds of *discrimination* are race, national or ethnic origin, color, religion, age, sex, sexual orientation, marital status, family status, disability and conviction for which a pardon has been granted.
- Harassment is any behavior that demeans, humiliates or embarrasses a person, and that a reasonable person should have known would be unwelcome. It includes actions (e.g. touching, pushing), comments (e.g. jokes, name-calling), or displays (e.g. posters, cartoons). *Sexual harassment* includes offensive or humiliating behavior that is related to a person's sex, as well as behavior of a sexual nature that creates an intimidating, hostile, or 'poisoned' work environment, or that could reasonably be thought to put sexual conditions on a person's job or employment opportunities. A few examples are: questions and discussions about a person's sexual life; touching a person in a sexual way; commenting on someone's sexual attractiveness or sexual unattractiveness; persisting in asking for a date after having been refused; telling a woman she belongs at home or is not suited for a particular job; eyeing someone in a suggestive way; displaying cartoons or posters of a sexual nature; writing sexually suggestive letters or notes.

## Workplace Rights

Read through the following list and note each item that you need to incorporate into your work day. Ask yourself, "Why haven't I believed I have this right? What am I afraid will happen if I assume this right?" Visualize yourself having this right and notice how you feel. Then act on it.

1. I have the right to be treated with respect and dignity.
2. I have the right to confront those who treat me with disrespect or abusive language or behavior.
3. I have the right to tell the truth about:
   – Those who treat me disrespectfully or abusively.
   – Situations that put my safety at risk.
   – Problems that affect my productivity or work satisfaction.
4. I have the right to be free of all *isms*—sexism, racism and ageism.
5. I have the right to refuse responsibility or blame for the actions and decisions of anyone except myself.
6. I have the right to ask for guidance and support.
7. I have the right to say, "I quit."

**Note**: You do not have the right to:
• Violate others' rights as described above.
• Be absent indiscriminately.
• Keep your job if you don't meet organizational expectations.

To protect yourself in future and potential disputes, record incidents of verbal abuse, harassment, sexual inappropriateness or any other invasive behaviors.

• Abuse of authority occurs when a person uses authority unreasonably to interfere with an employee or the employee's job. It includes humiliation, intimidation, threats, and coercion. It does not include normal managerial activities, such as counseling, performance appraisals, and discipline, as long as these are not being done in a discriminatory manner.
• Each employee has the right to be treated fairly and respectfully in the workplace. Each employee also has the responsibility to treat co-workers and customers in a way that respects individual differences.

# II
# Nurture Your WOWness

> *The optimist sees problems as opportunities and knows she has the skills to care for herself and to deal with what is hard.*

- Put Pollyanna to Shame: Think Optimistically
- Sweet-Talk to Yourself
- Honor Your Feelings
- Move Out of Painful Feelings
- Have a *Good* Cry
- Lighten Up!
- Attend to Your Body

## 1. Put Pollyanna to Shame: Think Optimistically

WE were in a heated argument when suddenly he yelled, "Stop being such a Pollyanna!" My optimistic tendency was evident and frustrating to my colleague's sensibility. Optimists tend to see the cheery side, to believe that people are doing the best they can, to picture success rather than failure. Those with a more pessimistic attitude tend to call those with optimism *naïve and out of touch with reality*. Yes, I've been called naïve as well.

*It's okay to be called Pollyanna. Sure beats the Nag from Hagerville.*

Those with a hefty dose of optimism tend to experience their pessimistic friends as discouraging and gloomy, as exemplified in this line from Michel de Saint-Pierre. "An optimist sees a light where there is none but why must the pessimist always run to blow it out?" To my delight, optimistic thinking showed up in surveys. Here are some samples of how resilient women used optimistic thinking as a WOW strategy:

- Life is too short to sweat the small stuff. Enjoy the now.
- Coped using positive self-talk.
- I can change how I react to people but I cannot change the other person.
- Good things sometimes come out of bad things.
- Feeling grateful.
- Every situation that has seemed the most difficult has brought me my greatest learning opportunities.

In 1990, Martin Seligman released his ground-breaking book, *Learned Optimism*. Since I have occasionally been accused of thinking and behaving like a Pollyanna, his work was of interest to me. Plus, it gave me some insights into light-hearted concepts. Seligman made a number of mental health-related findings.

### When Life Goes Miserably

Seligman describes pessimism as a habit of explaining painful life happenings as permanent, all-encompassing and personal. Pessimists tend to use words like *always* and *never* and phrases such as, "I'll never succeed," "I'll always be at the bottom of the garbage bin." Their optimistic neighbor, with the mantra of, "This too shall pass," speaks with words like *sometimes* and *recently* and phrases such as, "Hey, so what? I sometimes make mistakes but I learn from them." Some people find optimists a tad irritating. While pessimists tend to generalize their disappointments, "All managers are bossy," optimists focus on specific incidents of discontent, "I felt discouraged when my manager told me to redo the report."

### When Life Goes Merrily

Explanations of happiness by pessimists are temporary. "Ah, it was a fluke. My competitor didn't know what she was doing so I got the contract." That's when those who exercise optimism give a permanent explanation based on their character or abilities: "With my talent, uniqueness, flexibility and charming character, I will continue to attract clients." Did I mention that optimists can be a tad irritating? But so are pessimists. That's true whenever a strength or quality is taken to an extreme. As Seligman states, "The optimistic explanatory style for good events is opposite to that for bad events. The optimist believes that bad events have specific causes, while good events will enhance everything he does; the pessimist believes that bad events have universal causes and that good events are caused by specific factors."

### Internal versus External

Seligman studied how pessimists tend to internalize responsibility when circumstances are negative. They think they are worthless, talentless and unlovable. They say things like, "I'm stupid. It's all my fault." They tend to blame others or circumstances outside themselves thinking, "They are so stupid; they don't know a good thing when they see it." In contrast, the danger of extreme optimism is the tendency to avoid responsibility for one's part in an unsuccessful event. However, pessimists' tendency to regularly and inappropriately accept responsibility is a sure formula for depression.

Based on positive psychology findings, there are a number of advantages to developing an optimistic perspective. Since it supports depression, pessimism is associated with a weak immune system. Pessimism feels down—blue, sad, worried or anxious. Optimism and pessimism can become self-fulfilling prophesies. Because pessimists tend not to create or face challenges, they fail more frequently—even when success is possible. Seligman says, "The best thing one can say about a pessimist is that his fears were founded."

Alternatively, optimism encourages happiness and, therefore, is associated with vitality. Optimism feels up—hopeful, confident and cheerful. I say, "The best thing one can say about an optimist is that she enjoyed the challenge regardless of the outcome."

Optimism needs restraint when the cost of failure of a choice is clearly too high. Then we need to slow down and look at reality. It may have been an optimist who invented the automobile and a pessimist who created the brakes and the air bag. However, it was Dr. Phillip McGraw who said, "Eighty percent of our decisions are based on fear." If that's true, we live in a pessimistic culture that could use some optimistic balancing. Here are some optimistic how to's:

- Realize your beliefs are just that—beliefs. They may or may not be factual.
- Ask if your beliefs are useful and supportive to your work and life.
- Argue with yourself. Say, "Stop!" to pessimistic self-talk and replace with some optimistic thinking. "I know enough. I do enough."
- Ask, "What's the worst that could happen? Do I have a strategy to deal with that outcome?" If not, create one.
- Do something for those less fortunate.
- Develop your optimism muscle by seeing the bright side. Change Bad News into Good News. "I don't like the extra weight on my hips but now there is more of me to love."
- Count your blessings.

Optimists and pessimists have been around since Noah. Was he a pessimist to believe the flood was coming or was he an optimist to believe his idea of an ark would help all those critters? Optimists are definitely known for their action and hope. Now consider these tips to more often think like an optimist.

## Ten Tips to Think Like an Optimist

*"I think I can. I know I can."*

1. Move like an optimist! It is impossible to feel depressed while smiling, walking briskly or dancing to happy music. The majority of songs are about unhappy topics. Throw them away so you don't brainwash yourself into feeling sad. Sing and dance to happy songs.
2. Self-talk can hurt or uplift you. You can look in the mirror and recite a long list of negative descriptions or you can look in the mirror and speak kindly to yourself. Think of how you would treat someone you care about and then treat yourself in that way.
3. Visualize your negative-thought gremlins and see yourself swooping them up in a canvas bag. Tie them up with mental ropes and fling those gremlins deep into the ocean. Then take a deep breath and feel free.
4. Spend five minutes when you first wake thinking about your blessings. Say them out loud. Feel grateful for the sun rising, your good health, a comfy mattress and pillow or the roof over your head when it rains. It doesn't matter what you are grateful for, it only matters that you are grateful. Dig deep and find five minutes worth of gratefulness each morning.
5. Write five sentences to ask yourself. Tape them on the bathroom mirror or put them someplace you'll see first thing in the morning. You might ask, "What could possibly happen today that will be *better* than what happened yesterday?" "What will I learn today that will help me grow in the direction of my goals?" These questions presuppose that something will happen to lead you the way you want to go.
6. Write a list of your life goals. You deserve to have a plan and not have life happen *to* you. Look for one of the dozens of books and teachers who show you effective ways to figure out your goals.
7. List everything you have accomplished from learning how to ride a bike to earning a PhD. Place it somewhere convenient so you can easily add to the list. The more the better. This list can be a life-long project.
8. Consider the influence of your friends and with whom you spend the most time. If people typically feel upbeat, they will lift you; if they typically feel angry or depressed, they will drag you down.

9. Read uplifting books like Jack Canfield's *The Success Principles* and actually do the suggested activities.

10. Look deep into a mirror. See your spirit and think about the saying, *You are not a human being having a spiritual experience, you are a spiritual being having a human experience.*

*Source:* JULIE DONNELLY

## 2. Sweet-Talk to Yourself

SOMETIMES life stinks. We suddenly discover that we've been drifting in a leaky boat that finally goes under. No matter how competent we are, events external to our locus of control can destroy what is important to us. Multiple adversities make crumbling into ashes *normal*. Yet, through adversity, a stronger woman emerges with increased self-esteem.

*We owe ourselves the resolve to channel our 12,000+ thoughts a day into supportive and optimistic self-talk.*

Self-esteem relies on the affirming messages we receive, accept and internalize. We do have the power to reject thoughts that are harmful to our well being. As John Milton said, "The mind is its own place, and can make a heaven of hell and a hell of heaven." The counselor and author, Rick Carson, described these negative messages or *stinking thinking* as originating from Gremlins, nasty little internal creatures whose nasty nattering beats up our psyche.

Consider that thoughts are like seeds that get planted in the mind or not. Once planted, we can decide to water them or weed them out. It was our eldest daughter, Kelly, who one day said something like, "We are not responsible for our initial thoughts. But we are responsible for how long we entertain them, act on them or don't." Nine survey respondents specifically identified affirming self-talk as their WOW strategy. One wrote, "I talked in my brain. 'I can handle this. Stay calm.'"

The power of nurturing or focusing on negative or positive thoughts is poignantly described in a North America aboriginal legend, *Two Wolves*.

An old Cherokee Grandfather, whose grandson came to him in anger over a friend who had done him an injustice, said:

"Let me tell you a story. I too, at times, have felt a great hate for those that have taken so much, with no sorrow for what they do.

"But hate wears you down, and does not hurt your enemy. It is like taking poison and wishing your enemy would die. I have struggled with these feelings many times."

He continued, "It is as if there are two wolves inside me; one is good and does no harm. He lives in harmony with all around him and does not take offense when no offense was intended. He will only fight when it is right to do so, and in the right way.

"But the other wolf, ah! He is full of anger. The littlest thing will set him into a fit of temper. He fights everyone, all the time, for no reason. He cannot think because his anger and hate are so great. It is helpless anger, for his anger will change nothing.

"It is hard to live with these two wolves inside me, for both of them try to dominate my spirit."

The boy looked intently into his Grandfather's eyes and asked "Which one wins, Grandfather?"

The Grandfather smiled and quietly said, "The one I feed."

If we linger on a thought, replay it repeatedly or if it hits us at a vulnerable moment or is uttered by a powerful role model, it can become rooted in our unconscious as a belief. Beliefs ground our actions. Let's break this process down:

1. **Situation**: Words are spoken or an event occurs that stimulates a thought.
2. **Belief**: If the thought or self-talk is frequently repeated, it becomes a core belief in the unconscious mind.
3. **Feeling**: The deeper the belief, the stronger the corresponding feeling state.
4. **Reaction**: Feelings generated in unconsciousness result in reactions rather than mindful responses.

Situation ➤ Unconscious Belief* ➤ Feeling ➤ Reaction
* Engrained by repeated thoughts

This pattern works for self-critical, self-put-down, self-judging, self-discouraging, self-attacking and self-blaming thoughts, as well as self-caring, self-affirming, self-esteem-building, self-appreciative, self-empathic and self-forgiving thoughts. When I was a child, my father called me *stupid* a number of times. I carried that belief through school—repeating an elementary grade and dropping out of high school. After leaving home, I continued the habit he taught me—of calling myself stupid. That word became a belief and part of my identity. I felt sad, stupid and incompetent. Each time I made a mistake as an adult, the whole internal process was triggered. It looked like this:

Situation ➤ Unconscious Belief * ➤ Feeling ➤ Reaction
* Engrained by repeated thought

Mistake ➤ "I am stupid"* ➤ Insecure ➤ Cry and give up
* I unconsciously give meaning to the event

It was René Descartes who said, "I think, therefore I am." My *I think* was "*I think I am stupid.*" The wonderful thing about becoming an adult is that we are responsible for our lives, including our thinking. My belief system reprogramming included "Cancel! Cancel! That was Dad's idea and I have a different thought and belief. I learn from mistakes." I said that over and over again to myself and watched different results until it was unconscious. Now, the pattern looks like this:

Situation ➤ Unconscious Belief* ➤ Feeling ➤ Reaction
* Give new meaning to engrained thought

Mistake ➤ "I learn from mistakes"* ➤ Empowered ➤ Refocus and do it!
* Work at engraining new and healthy thought

What about you? What negative and false thoughts were programmed into your mind and have been rooted as painful mantras in your head? The publisher, Robert Collier, said, "Any thought that is passed on to the subconscious often enough and convincingly enough is finally accepted." The good news is that the unconscious can be reprogrammed by awareness and effort.

Consider noticing your self-talk. Anchor and reinforce your supportive messages. They're the brain's *good guys*. Watch yourself at work and home. Notice when it is hard to think clearly. Identify the destructive thoughts, beliefs and chatter—the brain's *bad guys*—then clear them out. Say to yourself, "*Stop!*" then repeat what you want to believe.

Here are some sample thought shifts to assist you:

| | | |
|---|---|---|
| • I am inadequate. | ➤ | • I do the best I can. |
| • I am not good enough. | ➤ | • I am as deserving as anyone else. |
| • I cannot trust my judgment. | ➤ | • I can learn to trust my judgment. |
| • I am a failure. | ➤ | • I have succeeded at… |
| • I am not in control. | ➤ | • I control my own actions. |
| • I am powerless. | ➤ | • I have choices. |
| • I am weak. | ➤ | • It's alright to sometimes feel weak. |
| • I am stupid. | ➤ | • I have (physical, emotional, mental, social, musical, mechanical or mathematical) intelligence. |
| • I am a disappointment. | ➤ | • I am okay just the way I am. |
| • I have to be perfect. | ➤ | • Making mistakes is okay. |
| • I did something wrong. | ➤ | • I can learn from my experience. |
| • I cannot trust others. | ➤ | • I can choose who to trust for what. |
| • It's not nice to say no. | ➤ | • I can say *yes, no* or *I want to think about it.* |

Be easy on yourself. Remember Dr. Siebert's caution of overdoing or forcing affirmations. If you've spent 15 or more years grooving some damaging thoughts into your unconscious mind, it will take significant time to delete and replace them. Newly inserted thoughts require cultivation, time and attention. Be persistent and vigilant. Start with one harsh belief. Write out your new and nurturing thought. Post it. No one at work need see it but you. Repeat it. Make healthy and vibrant action choices based on your improved mind set. As a pioneer in positive thinking, Norman Vincent Peale said, "Change your thoughts and you change your world." I add, "Change your thoughts and you strengthen your resilience on the job and elsewhere."

## 3. Honor Your Feelings

THE Oxford dictionary defines *feeling* to mean "to touch or have an emotion" and *emotion* as "the feeling part of awareness as compared to thinking." As discussed above in *Sweet-Talk to Yourself*, feelings are typically responses to our thoughts and beliefs. Most of our misery is created by stinking thinking or damaging self-talk often implanted in our early years. Consider the message my Dad gave me about being stupid that created the reaction of insecurity to making mistakes. Of course, if a child believes

*You need your mind to figure out the world and your feelings to figure out yourself. That's using your emotional smarts.*

she has lost the support of her parent, she will understandably feel insecure. As a child, the feeling was appropriate to the situation and message. But, as an adult, the stinking-thinking reaction is inappropriate. When we lose our ability to think clearly, we are triggered psychologically into the past and are literally reliving an old feeling.

Authentic feelings are those that were present when you were a baby, clear of damaging messages. *Baby* feelings are body responses that act like a thermometer to inform you about your unique likes, desires and wants. Imagine caring for a baby. Listen to the sound of:

- the *sad* cry with the message that she doesn't have what she needs. She needs her diaper changed.
- the *scared* cry when a stranger comes to change her diaper. She fears the loss of her most beloved parent. She needs to be assured that she is safe.
- the *hurt* cry when the diaper pin (accidentally, of course) pricks her skin and causes pain.
- the *mad* cry, a secondary emotion, which tells her she has the energy to get what she wants, her mother.
- the *glad* coo when mother appears. Baby has what she wants!

Why is anger a secondary emotion? Typically, we feel sad, hurt or scared before anger kicks in. The baby tries to meet her needs first with a softer sad, scared or hurt cry. If those needs aren't met, she will up the volume with a LOUD, demanding scream: "It's survival mom!" Especially when the bottle doesn't come. Our baby is in trouble if she stops crying for her needs.

Those who struggle with expressing anger appropriately benefit from slowing down their reaction and asking, "What do I feel first?" In healthy relationships, we ideally get our needs met in the sad, hurt or scared/concerned realm before having to fire up feeling and expressing fury.

If all babies feel sad, hurt, scared, mad or glad, why is that grown men and women appear to have different capacities in expressing them? Dr. William Pollack coined the phrase *The Boy Code* to explain that boys (remember there are exceptions) are socialized out of feeling and expressing vulnerable feelings. Boys are at risk of being called nasty names like *wuss*, *wimp* and *girl* (as if that is a derogatory term), particularly by their sports coach, if they show any sign of feeling sad, hurt or scared. So, they typically swallow their tears or are shamed with, "Big boys don't cry." What does that leave the socialized male to express? Anger or happiness! No wonder your male co-worker or boss becomes more aggressive when faced with vulnerable feelings. He doesn't have experience identifying, experiencing or managing them in himself, let alone expressing them to someone else. He's left in the even more uncomfortable position of helplessness.

In the meantime, little girls have typically (remember there are exceptions) been socialized to avoid expressing anger. "It's not ladylike. It's not nice." Since anger is the energy to help you get what you want and need, for generations women have been dependent on men, their knights in shining armor and saviors, to rescue them, the damsels in distress. Just watch a Jane Austin movie to see this dynamic played out. The suffragettes of the 1920s and the feminists of the 1970s were seen as out-of-control women because they courageously expressed anger.

Consequently, we have learned in myriad ways to confuse our core, natural or baby feelings with unconscious adult reactions.

The trick is to separate old, triggered and inappropriate reactions from present-moment feelings. When you are triggered by an event or remark, ask yourself, "How old do I feel?" If you feel like a two-year-old, excuse yourself and sort out how much this has to do with your past and how much has to do with the present situation. Note what you are feeling and what, if anything, you need. For example, "When you are at work do you feel:

1. enlivened?
2. neutral?
3. burned out?

If your answer is *enlivened*, that personal information affirms the good fit of your workplace. If your answer is *neutral*, you may ask yourself, "What can I do differently to feel *enlivened* by my work?" If your answer is *burned out*, you need to ask yourself, "What do I need to do differently to look after myself?" You might consider engaging with a supportive and listening friend or seeking help from a professional.

## 4. Move Out of Painful Feelings

THE questions in the previous section illustrate how authentic feelings inform us of what we want, what is important to us, what we value, what is working for us and what is not. At the same time, feelings tell little, if nothing, about other people or the external world. We need our fine brains and observation skills to figure out our external life. Feelings are experienced through the body's systems of muscles, nerves and organs. We all have the ability to feel emotions but we each feel differently about different aspects of life. My hubby feels excited and energized just thinking about wilderness canoeing while I feel disgruntled and bored at the thought of the isolation. I feel excited and energized just thinking of attending a personal growth retreat while he feels disinterested.

*"I can learn to contain and appreciate how I feel."*

Here is the paradox of all feelings. Once you are in a feeling state, it does not work to critically beat yourself up, dismiss the feeling or push it into your pantyhose. The feeling will actually increase if it is not acknowledged. Have you ever been told, "Don't cry!" and then the tears come on even heavier? Unlike critical thoughts that are useful to challenge, feelings only calm once they are totally felt, experienced and often shared.

Any time we are in a high-feeling state, our ability to think clearly is minimized. Imagine encountering a mama grizzly bear. You probably tell yourself, "Darn! I could die!" Your muscles contract, your heart rate accelerates and adrenalin kicks in. You are in high alert, high fear. But it doesn't take a bear to create this reaction. You might feel dread of a co-worker's or manager's feedback. Once the trigger is pulled, it requires awareness and self-care to bring yourself to a neutral and rational state. Feel the feeling, notice your breath and calm yourself while remembering you're a grown up with choices. The energy in the feeling actually *lets go*. Pushing away or ignoring the feeling does not work.

The body can actually break down or at least cause physical pain if the feeling is stuffed. Hence, the power of listening skills to shift a feeling state. Sounds complicated? It can be. Accessing counseling or therapy can help turn this description into an understandable experience. In the meantime, here are steps to follow if you become triggered by events and overwhelmed by feelings:

1. Accept the feeling as it is. Breathe and notice the feeling in your body. It's optional if you give the feeling a label such as *sad* or *hurt*.
2. Notice how old you feel. Breathe some more.
3. Tell yourself, "It's only a feeling. It will pass."

Once you feel calm and your brain is able to function:

1. Decide if this strong feeling was sparked by old programming or is *clean*.
2. Notice what thought or belief is behind the feeling. Is it appropriate to the situation? Is it true? Is it more of a judgment or assumption than an observation of facts?
3. Use your problem-solving brain to decide if action is required.

## Body/Feeling Awareness

| Low State | | High State |
|---|---|---|
| DOWN | **SAD** | MISERABLE |
| BLAH | ⬅III  III➡ DISCOURAGED | DEPRESSED |

BODY MESSAGE: You *do not have* what you want, need or value.

| DISAPPOINTED | **HURT** | CRUSHED |
|---|---|---|
| BELITTLED | ⬅III  III➡ PAINED | DESTROYED |

BODY MESSAGE: What you want, need or value has been *taken away*.

| UNEASY | **AFRAID** | TERRIFIED |
|---|---|---|
| TROUBLED | ⬅III  III➡ SCARED | DESPERATE |

BODY MESSAGE: What you want, need or value
is *at risk* of being taken away.

| AGITATED | **ANGRY** | BITTER |
|---|---|---|
| IRRITATED | ⬅III  III➡ EXASPERATED | HOSTILE |

BODY MESSAGE: You have *the energy to acquire* what you want,
need or value (secondary emotion).

| CONTENT | **HAPPY** | THRILLED |
|---|---|---|
| PLEASED | ⬅III  III➡ GLAD | ECSTATIC |

BODY MESSAGE: You *have* what you want, need or value.

The basic feelings are sad, hurt, afraid, angry and happy. They have a range of weak to strong energy with dozens of words to describe them. Many of them describe the state of our body with words such as down, tight, deflated, empty, uneasy, agitated, up, energized, pumped or high. Review the model opposite to enhance your awareness of feelings.

How is this feeling information going to help you at work? Daniel Goleman wrote in *Emotional Intelligence: Why It Can Matter More Than IQ*, "Emotional intelligence is the capacity for recognizing our own feelings and those of others, for motivating ourselves and for managing emotions well in ourselves and in our relationships."

## 5. Have a *Good* Cry

MY friend, Sandy, yelled, "Don't cry on me. Please don't! I can't stand it if you cry!" I felt sadder. We just had a significant disagreement and I felt disconnected from her. I felt tightness in my stomach and a constriction of my heart. Crying is the baby's natural response when his or her needs are not met. Regrettably, we have been socialized out of our appreciation for a *good cry*. When I was leading a professional development seminar, a young career woman asked me, "How can you stop yourself from crying in front of your boss?" My thought was, "How sad," as I recalled releasing tears in front of *safe managers* and, as a manager, supporting others as they cried in front of me.

*There's nothing to fear about a tear.*

The biochemist, William Frey, author of *Crying: The Mystery of Tears*, concluded that nearly one half of tears shed are letting go of sadnes. Sometimes tears express fear, anxiety, anger and even extreme happiness. Many of us cry until we laugh or laugh until we cry. Frey also concluded that tears, along with perspiration, urine and exhalation rid our bodies of toxins and other waste.

Yet, our culture has strong taboos about crying. "Don't be a wimp!" "He broke down." "She couldn't hold it together," and the famous Donald Trump line, "You're fired…especially if you cry!" One of my favorite movies is *Bridges of Madison County*. I felt thrilled when Clint Eastwood, famed for his Dirty Harry crime movies and other tough and rough roles, stood in the rain weeping over the loss of his love, Meryl Streep. Another favorite moment is watching Robin William's tears in the movie, *Mrs. Doubtfire*. Our culture benefits from seeing the realness of emotions in both men and women.

Yet, there's such fear of crying that women are accused of manipulating others with the use of tears. Maybe some do but I am convinced most don't. I'll never forget receiving the declaration, "You are using your tears to control us," from a social worker during a family therapy session when I was nursing my newborn baby. I was recovering from surgery and feeling sleep deprived. My tears said, "I give up. I have nothing left inside to give." Over the years, I have repeatedly witnessed the same reality from hundreds of other women I have supported.

Fifteen survey respondents referred to crying as part of their worst workplace experience. One survey respondent described her reaction to a critical comment, "I cried! Darn it!" So what's a woman supposed to do if she has a boss who overtly or covertly enforces a crying ban?

Here are some suggestions:

- If it is risky for your manager to witness tears, breathe deeply, feel your feet on the floor and look up towards the ceiling. Looking down tends to take us deeper into feelings.
- Another option is to imagine a bubble around yourself. As you breathe in, focus on strengthening your solar plexus or inner core. These first two strategies help you contain tears until you can take them somewhere emotionally safe.
- If containing the tears is just too much, say, "Excuse me, I will be back in five minutes." Go have your cry, blow your nose and drink some water.
- When it is safe to do so, find a caring person and/or place to have a good cry. Let it out.
- If the tears are stuck in your stomach, chest or throat, have a bubble bath, watch a tender movie, read old love letters or curl up on your sweetie's lap. Relax until you can weep.
- Don't swallow tears.

As my mentor, Gwendolyn Jansma, says, "Better to cry on the outside than drown on the inside."

Crying leads us into a discussion about grieving. Fifteen survey respondents identified the death of a co-worker, friend or family member as their greatest Woe factor. Another 13 identified being fired or let go. They are all describing *loss*. A survey respondent wrote about her greatest challenge as, "the sudden death of my 44-year-old sister." It doesn't matter if your loss is your job, your parent or your cat. Significant

## Ten Tips for Grieving

*"Good grief! I need a good cry."*

1. Allow yourself to feel.
2. Take your grief to those who can listen without judgment or a need to fix you. Grief support groups are often very helpful.
3. Notice if you have unresolved issues with your loss of a family member, a pet, friend, job or status.
4. Forgive yourself if you hadn't made an effective closure with someone.
5. Write a letter of goodbye to those involved—even if they have already passed on.
6. Take bereavement leave or not. You decide what your emotional needs are.
7. Forgive those who say, "I know how you feel." While they don't know, their intention is to support you.
8. Consider taking action—donate to a foundation or commission a park bench with their name—to give meaning to your loss.
9. Realize that for big losses you may never return totally to the way you were.
10. Support yourself with positive memories.

change has happened to you. Loss is a reminder that there are areas of life you don't have control over. Thirty years ago, Elisabeth Kubler-Ross provided a framework for the topic of death, grieving and loss with her classic book, *On Death and Dying*. She proposed five steps to the grief process:

- Denial—*This isn't happening.*
- Anger—*Why is this happening to me?*
- Bargaining—*I promise I'll change if…*
- Depression—*I give up.*
- Acceptance—*I'm alright.*

In psychological circles, it is well accepted that these reactions may not happen in a linear timeline. We all manage loss differently and most of us never completely recover from a major loss. Regardless, when we're reeling from a loss, we can expect to feel some numbness and disorientation.

I observed my mother recover from the death of my father and our son struggle with the loss of his dream marriage when his first wife became ill and died from cancer. In contrast to our son, we never saw my mother in an angry, depressed or bargaining state. She saw life unfold and move in its expected form; you live as fully as you can, get older and then death comes. Our son, on the other hand, felt robbed and, in moments of despair, would ask, "Why me?" and "Why us?" Grieving is a personal matter; one that can take a toll at home and work. Few workplaces, regrettably, offer ample or flexible bereavement leave. While for some a supportive workplace is the best place to be after a loss, others may require a leave of a month or more. Take the best possible care of yourself when you need to grieve. Remember, no one knows exactly the sorrow you feel.

## 6. Lighten Up!

RESEARCHERS report a number of health benefits of laughter. Stress is reduced, blood pressure is lowered, the immune system is strengthened, creativity increases, mood is elevated and muscles relax. Actually, you cannot restrict your muscles when you either laugh or cry. So, laugh until you cry or cry until you laugh. On top of all the health benefits, people enjoy connecting to someone with a lighthearted approach. However, having a sense of humor does not necessarily mean you are known for rousing others into ripples of laughing convulsion.

*The goddesses may be giggling at how seriously we take ourselves.*

Linda Bradburn, along with six survey respondents, uses humor as a useful tool to keep a lighter perspective on life's inevitable grumbles, grunts and bumps. Even the willingness to smile can be helpful. As one respondent wrote, "A smile goes a long way. It puts people on a good footing with you." Developing a sense of humor merely requires the ability to look at life from a different and fun perspective. Those that use it look to friends to share a good laugh or find ways to not take themselves so seriously. You can be the initiator of a humorous perspective or the appreciative recipient—the humorist or the humored.

Most of us, at some time or other, crack a smile, if not a gut-wrenching guffaw. You can begin by identifying your favorite smile makers as an indication of your humor preferences. Professional humorists range from comic strip and cartoon creators to stand-up comics, from late-night show hosts to writers and philosophers. They use language that includes exaggeration, irony, satire, over-literalness, jokes, fun lists, and word plays like riddles, rhymes and puns. They may employ observational incongruities, self-deprecation, insults, mimicking, storytelling and slapstick. Their presentation style may be eccentric, angry, gross, rude, child-like or idiot-like. Content is endless, although politics and sex are two favorites.

It is still considered lady-like behavior, by many, to politely laugh at any male-delivered, even sexist, jokes. If offended, some assertive women will not laugh or will bravely say, "That's not funny." Dolly Parton provides a moderate, self-deprecating yet effective example, "I'm not offended by all the dumb blonde jokes because I know I'm not dumb...and I also know I'm not blonde."

In fact, Canadian psychology professor, Herbert Lefcourt, discovered that women gain more health benefits from using humor as a means of coping than men. "Our suspicion is that women's coping humor takes the form of laughing at themselves, which restores social closeness. Men's coping humor takes the forms of attacking others, which represents an attempt to maintain their position in the social hierarchy." Hence, the more frequent use of put-down and sarcastic humor by men.

Professor of Women's Literature, Dr. Regina Barreca, refers to the *Humane Humor Rule*. She observes that seldom do women make fun of what people cannot change—physical appearance, sex, sexual orientation or race. Humorist, Liz Curtis Higgs, said, "Women love to laugh at themselves, but men seem to laugh at the other guy." A research study by J.B. Levine in the *Journal of Communication* reported that 63 percent of the humor used by women included self-disparaging comments, compared to only 12 percent by males. However, in *What Mona Lisa Knew: A Woman's Guide to Getting Ahead in Business by Lightening Up*, Dr. Barbara Mackoff warns us gals that, if we over-use self-deprecating humor, we can create the impression of incompetence.

Note the gentler references by women to the opposite sex and the use of self-deprecation in the following joke examples:

**Men say:**

"Bachelors know more about women than married men; if they didn't, they'd be married too."                                      — HENRY LOUIS MENCKEN

"Bachelors should be heavily taxed. It is not fair that some men should be happier than others."                                              — OSCAR WILDE

"I don't think I'll get married again. I'll just find a woman I don't like and give her a house."
— LEWIS GRIZZARD

**Women say:**

"The only time a woman really succeeds in changing a man is when he's a baby."
— NATALIE WOOD

"Sex when you're married is like going to a 7-Eleven. There's not as much variety, but at three in the morning, it's always there."
— CAROL LEIFER

"Men have higher body temperatures than women. If your heating goes out in winter, I recommend sleeping next to a man. Men are like portable heaters that snore."
— RITA RUDNER

Mackoff offers a humor strategy for replying to sexual stereotyping and conflict-triggering comments. She suggests responding as if the speaker was intending to make a joke. One example Mackoff offers is, if told something like, "Women belong home with their kids," look surprised and quip, "Say, that's a new one?!"

Humor can help you sustain a more positive, upbeat attitude while dealing with daily hassles. Every now and then, reflect on different situations and ask if you just might have taken yourself a little too seriously. It might be time to lighten up!

## 7. Attend to Your Body

MILLIONS of dollars worth of books fill the health sections of bookstores with basically the same message—get adequate rest, exercise more and eat less. We have loads of information about making wise wellness decisions. One of my favorite books is *You: The Owner's Manual*, by Dr. Michael Roizen and Dr. Mehmet Oz.

Regardless of the volumes of health-related information, most of our ailments are created through poor care of our bodies. Eight survey respondents reported that they had created poor health. One survey respondent wrote, "I was so miserable I put my health on the back burner."

I have done my fair share of bodily harm through neglect. Mostly, I've mended my habits. I've learned that those with high resistance to illness recognize and pay attention to distress. They have routines and habits that create wellbeing and relaxation.

> *Your body doesn't lie.*
> *Listen to it.*

Two women reported their WOW strategy as, 'Trust my own instincts when it comes to my own body and health care," and "I forced myself to get out of bed early and go for a walk every day." The body responds with appreciation when given care and can respond with crippling results if not.

A useful and easy habit that has made a significant difference to me and many others is to identify beginning body symptoms—those small internal whispers that warn you of an impending and louder strain. Pay attention before you collapse or have a *heart attack*. There are more than 100 signals of body distresses. Here are some of the more common signals:

- Tension headaches
- Fatigue
- Colds
- Insomnia
- Teeth grinding
- Eye twitching

When the question arises, "What do I do with the stress in my body?" many people take time off from work, make appointments for a massage (still a good idea) and hang on until a holiday (not a good idea). Not long ago, stress researchers made a significant discovery. You can reduce your distress and "actual" age by attending to your body on a regular and daily basis, sometimes as often as every hour on a particularly challenging day. After locating tension in your body, systematically *Let Go*. Checking in regularly throughout the day and releasing the body tension provides relief. The Canadian Institute of Stress found when people took a "short amount of time *each day* to be good to themselves, [they] reduced their stress levels *by almost half.*"

I call this *be good to yourself* or body tension releasing, *30 Second Quickies*. They take 30 seconds or less to do. Note those items below that you do and will do to take care of yourself intermittently throughout your day:

- Yawn
- Wiggle
- Laugh or cry

- Slowly eat a grape
- Do a neck and shoulder roll
- Shake your right hand, then your left hand
- Stretch up, down, left and right
- Drink a glass of water
- Watch one breath go in and out
- Tighten your teeth and then relax your jaw
- Massage your scalp
- Squeeze your face into a prune shape
- Stick your tongue way out
- Kick off your shoes
- Yell (especially into a pillow or in your car)
- Sit down and lift your legs in the air
- Get or give a hug

# III
# Communicate with WOW Power

*The way you walk, talk and shop says a lot.*

- Be a Dear with Two Ears: Listen
- Speak Up: Assert or You'll Blurt
- Breathe and Get Grounded
- Ease Conflict
- Plan for Resolution
- Filter Criticism: Offer Feedback
- Manage Management

## 1. Be a Dear with Two Ears: Listen

THE motivational speaker, Zig Ziglar, once said, "People often say that motivation doesn't last. Well, neither does bathing—that's why we recommend it daily." The same philosophy holds true for listening, whether in intimate, family or working-relationship interactions. Over and over again, attending to other's messages is crucial for successful relationships. Only seven survey respondents described using listening to work through or face an adversity. One woman reported that when "team members were burning out, there was a rippling effect on the team." She "listened, created new opportunities for them when able based on needs, said *no* more consistently and let things go." Listening can be a powerful remedy to other's discontent. Alternatively, lack of listening can create disconnect and loss of respect.

*"It's an honor to be asked. Talk away."*

Years ago, I weakened a friendship. My friend came by train for a weekend visit. With my typical enthusiasm, I shared with her many aspects of my life explaining all the details from the story behind planting the tulips to how I had successfully toilet trained our youngest child. Then, I shared some more and some more. To her credit, once back in her own home, she wrote me a letter telling me how she left feeling invisible, unappreciated and disconnected. After buckets of tears, I vowed I would learn to listen.

Through a caring ear, others will sense that we respect them, are present and are safe for the sharing. The old cliché, *it is useful to have a sounding board*, is true. The late poet and author, Alice Duer Miller, described it like this, "You can listen like a blank wall or like a splendid auditorium where every sound comes back fuller and richer." Sometimes, we need a mirror, someone to witness our struggle or joy, someone to witness who we are.

As described in *Honor Your Feelings* on page 112, when we are in a high feeling state, there is little energy to fuel clear thinking. The brain goes on automatic pilot. Some people appear to flip into another personality. Jane might suddenly turn into Anxious Anne, Angry Agnes, or Suffering Sally. Listening helps bring people's brains back to a functioning mode. Don't ask a sobbing or fist-clenched employee when a report will be complete. Listen first.

Few of us know how to really listen. Here are some facts:

- 75 percent of the time, we are distracted, preoccupied or forgetful.
- More than 35 business studies indicate that listening is a top skill needed for success in business.
- Less than two percent of us have had formal education about listening.

*Source*: TRINITY COLLEGE

Most of us have blocks to effective listening. We may become triggered by elevated feeling states and begin to argue rather and listen. Argue with a person's feelings and those feelings may escalate into feeling frustrated or even enraged. People who feel heard and validated tend to calm.

Another tendency is to jump to the conclusion that a described problem is *our problem*. We take on the *problem ownership*. "What did I do wrong? What didn't I do? What am I supposed to do differently?" Many of us snap into fixing other's problems. Sometimes we take over and sometimes we give inappropriate or uninvited advice.

How do we begin to listen with empathy, not with apathetic uncaring demeanor nor with smothering "poor you, pity you" messages? First, we can begin with Stephen Covey's most quoted phrase of "seek first to understand the other." It is the seeking that is key to offering our attention and presence. This search does not require us to agree with the feelings or beliefs of the speaker. It does require openness. I once heard it said, "If you are not willing to change your mind, you are not really listening." That's especially true when engaged in disagreement or conflict.

### Basic Listening Steps

- **Step 1**:
  Sit down so that you can both be attentive and relaxed. Indicate you are listening with open body language and words like, "I'm listening."
- **Add Silence**…

- **Step 2**:
  Now and then say, "Thank you," or "Okay," or "Tell me more."
  When you don't understand say, "I don't understand."
  (or "Help me understand.")
  **Add**… "Please tell me that in a different way."
- **Add Silence**…

## Ten Tips for Listening

*"My ears are open and I'm here for you."*

1. Start from the standpoint that this is not your problem. Problem ownership belongs to the speaker.
2. Imagine yourself as a *sounding board*, mirror or witness to the speaker's struggles and joys.
3. Check that you are free of mental or physical distractions.
4. Check if this is a good time for you and the speaker. If not, agree on a convenient time.
5. Avoid arguing, consoling, pitying, fixing and analyzing.
6. Simply ask, "What do you want me to do—Simply listen or are you interested in some insights?"
7. Keep questions to a minimum and use them to clarify understanding. Questions can trigger the speaker into moving too quickly from feeling into thinking.
8. Listen and question with an attitude of curiosity in seeking to understand.
9. Force yourself not to fill in silent spaces.
10. If and when a friend gives you the gift of listening, express appreciation. Say, "Thank you for listening."

- **Step 3**:
  Add to **Step 2**. When you hear emotion in the voice, *catch* the word or phrase associated with the feeling and say, "Tell me..."
  Example: "Tell me more about doing it all alone."
- **Add Silence**...

- **Optional**: Those with a strong feeling vocabulary can help the speaker by guessing what feelings may be under the words. "Sounds like you are feeling sad." Feelings tell us everything about what is important to us but little about how to manage the world. The best of listening helps the speaker discover his or her inner world of thoughts and feelings.

- **Optional**: Ask a few open-ended questions using *how, who, what, when* and *where* to help you follow the speaker's story. Be careful not to ask a lot of questions as they tend to take us back into thinking mode. To begin, we want the speaker to engage with their internal feelings. Questions, however, can be very helpful once we are ready to think about solutions.

- **Optional**: When feelings calm, summarize in one sentence the problem or theme. "Sounds like you don't feel valued here."

- **Optional**: When feelings calm, invite the speaker to problem solve. Ask, "Do you want to talk about some solutions to this problem?"
  You may be rewarded with one of the most appreciative compliments ever: "Thank you for listening."

## 2. Speak Up: Assert or You'll Blurt

ONE strong trend in responses to my survey was regret for not standing up or speaking out about aggressive or abusive behaviors. Not one woman expressed regret for acting in an aggressive manner but many regretted their passivity when targeted for ill treatment. Here is some of what they learned:

- To be less tolerant of bad behavior.
- I can stand up for what is right.
- Keep your own power. Do what you can.
- To fight for myself and not let anyone bully me.
- I wish I'd stood up to her.
- To expect courtesy and respect from all relationships. Look after myself.
- Believe in yourself. Take a stand. Say what you feel.
- It is better to stick up for yourself and be called a "b#$%#" than be a doormat and be bullied.
- The value of being true to myself and seeking to resolve conflict constructively rather than avoiding it.
- I didn't make the world a better place by running away.

Consider the assertiveness skills model as an augmentation to *Establish Clear Boundaries* on pages 87–91. When you assert yourself, you are being yourself *on purpose*.

The purpose is to express respect for yourself and those with whom you have contact. When we act like a door mat, we violate our own rights. When we act aggressively like a bulldozer, we violate others' rights. The two keys are to speak up with *I* messages and to listen attentively. *Listening Skills* are described on page 128. We will focus here on the *speaking up* aspect.

*Feel the fear and speak up anyway. If you speak the truth you will at least have supported yourself.*

Most of us have a tendency to react in a passive, aggressive or passive/aggressive manner. As noted from the survey respondents, women traditionally lean towards passive or passive/aggressive behavior. Passive/aggressive behavior puts others in a double bind with a mixed message. "I'm in big trouble because of what you did but don't help me solve it. I'll suffer quietly." It sounds passive with an aggressive undertone. The chart on pages 132 – 133 summarizes the differences between acting passively, assertively or aggressively.

1. Decide if you tend to use passive, aggressive, passive/aggressive or assertive behaviors.
2. If you tend to act passively:
   - Take adult responsibility. Decide what you really want and take action.
   - Keep agreements. If someone helps, do your part by following through.
   - Ask yourself, "How can I get what I really want in a healthy way?"
   - Count your blessings. Acknowledge your strengths and what is going well.
   - Remember, *you make you*. Minimize self pity and take action.
3. If you tend to act aggressively:
   - Give up believing you have power over other people.
   - Listen to others. Really listen.
   - Make expectations clear. "I want this completed by Tuesday."
   - Practice asking others, "What do you need from me?"

Take the assertive position by making boundary declarations as described on page 89. Also begin to use the words *yes*, *no* and *it depends* in conscious ways. Be discerning and choose wisely. Please note that while a woman and a man may speak and act in a similar and assertive manner, the woman will be more likely accused of acting aggressively. Be aware of this societal bias.

## Ten Tips to Crimp Crummy Workplace Gossip

*"I heard from Lois that Mary said that Jane is messing around with the boss."*

1. If you participate in negative gossip ask yourself what is really going on for you. Do you feel jealous, resentful or superior? Does it give you a sense of belonging? What is the payoff for participating? Then find a healthy way to meet your need.

2. When you hear negative gossip about someone and it is untrue, say, "Interesting. That's not my experience."

3. Decide if you have the confidence to say, "What you're saying sounds negative and gossipy. I feel uncomfortable participating."

4. When you hear gossip about others, tell yourself, "I'm hearing one side of a story."

5. Rumors are rumors. Take them as such. Remember the telegraph game we played as kids? A sentence is whispered into one person's ear and is then passed from ear to another ear around a circle. Something like, "The pussy cat caught a mouse," can end up being, "Her messy hair was cut."

6. If the negative gossip is about you, consider the advantages and disadvantages of confronting the key gossiper.

7. If you address the person spreading the rumor and she retorts, "But I didn't say anything like that," merely, respond with, "Great, I'm glad to hear that."

8. Learn who can keep confidential and private information and who is the organizational blabbermouth.

9. Announce loud and clear your accomplishments and successes, particularly to the blabbermouth. You want this kind of rumor passed on.

10. Model practicing the fine art of Positive Gossip. You will gain a reputation of being an excellent networker.

There is an additional way I encourage you to speak up. Gossip! But only in the positive. Catty gossip is a dangerous pre-occupation and can create a toxic workplace. I've endured my share of gossip, that is, before having some strategies that turn the conversation around. After listening to critical and judgmental comments by a colleague about other colleagues, I am left wondering, "What does she say about *me* when I'm not around?" If you are guilty of mean-spirited gossip, ask yourself, "What need does this activity fill?" Then find healthy ways to meet it.

|  | **PASSIVE** *Gives up relationship with self* |
|---|---|
| **BELIEF** | • I have no rights<br>• You have all the rights |
| **BEHAVIOR** | • Acts like a martyr or victim<br>• Is submissive<br>• Defers to others<br>• Does not express wants, ideas or feelings<br>• Expresses self in an apologetic manner |
| **INTENTION & GOALS** | • To please and get love, acceptance or approval<br>• To be liked and avoid conflict at all costs |
| **EMOTIONAL STATE** | • Low self-esteem<br>• Feelings of high anxiety, powerlessness, frustration, resentment, being used and hopelessness |
| **HOW OTHERS FEEL** | • Frustrated, pity, angry, guilty or resentful |
| **PAYOFFS** | • Avoids confrontations, risk of disapproval or being seen as wrong |

Adapted from: Jakubowski, P. & Lange, A. (1978). *The assertive option*. Champaign, IL: Research Press.

| ASSERTIVE | AGGRESSIVE |
|---|---|
| | *Gives up relationship with others* |
| • Our rights and wants are equally important | • I have all the rights <br> • You have no rights |
| • Expresses own beliefs feelings and wants in an open, honest, direct and appropriate manner <br> • Listens, shares and exchanges information <br> • Is willing to be influenced <br> • Uses "I" messages | • Sacrifices others <br> • Blames others to win <br> • Name calls and yells <br> • Puts others down <br> • Threatens <br> • Expresses wants, ideas and feelings at the expense of others |
| • To communicate <br> • To develop healthy give and take relationships while not always getting own way | • To dominate and control <br> • To protect self at all cost |
| • Healthy self-esteem <br> • Feelings of confidence and hope | • Feelings of self-righteousness and power <br> • Powerlessness, guilt and embarrassment |
| • Trusted, trusting, respected, respectful, heard, seen and understood | • Fearful, hurt, resentful or angry. |
| • Self confidence <br> • Influence and respect <br> • Healthier relationships | • Short term illusion of control and power <br> • Feelings released <br> • Others' compliance <br> • Note: Relationships are painful or destroyed |

The practice of Positive Gossip is what I advocate. It creates wonderful connections with people. Try this. The next time you hear something complimentary about a friend or colleague, make sure to pass it on, especially to the source of the good news. "Sally, I met your new manager. He's thrilled with your organizational skills." Guess what? This kind of comment is powerful. When we hear a direct compliment, we sometimes think, "Ahh, nice and she's being polite." When we hear positive gossip, the information through the grapevine, we're apt to give it more weight.

## 3. Breathe and Get Grounded

WHAT happens when two people are having a rational, calm discussion and then *Wham! Bam!* one of them is red in the face, talking in an incoherent or angry rant? It's hard to tell the difference between them and an overgrown two-year-old having a temper tantrum or a sulk. Here are some descriptions of similar moments from survey respondents:

- Blew up, screamed and cried at my boss.
- Cried, screamed.
- A lot of tears, apologies, trying to rebuild trust.

"Sometimes I feel dragged into a helpless and scared two-year-old's body."

What happens when adults regress to acting like infants is that tears sometimes erupt and emotional buttons are triggered. It's like many of us walk around with sensitive buttons or switches on our chests which can be accidentally activated. The more disturbing our life events, typically, the more and bigger the trigger buttons.

Picture this. Someone says something in a voice louder than usual. Your don't-push-me-around button is triggered. Your chin begins to wobble; you try to swallow your tears; words blurt out and the regression begins. "How could you say that? I won't let you talk to me like that…*blah, blah, blah!*"

If this seems familiar, don't be hard on yourself. You're human and were triggered into reaction rather than response, triggered into acting much younger than your years. Consider what David Richo, author of *How to be an Adult in Relationships*, says, "We are born with a capacity to dance together but not with the necessary training. We have to learn the dance steps and practice until we move with ease and grace." Here are some strategies to regain and retain adult status.

### When You Become Triggered

1. Develop a witness, a part of you that can benevolently watch over you. It will notice when an old and negative message or tape in your head is triggered and released. It becomes an internal voice that really cares and brings you back to sanity. It might even have a sense of humor. Instead of "Woe" say, "Whoa Horsey! This is going poorly."
2. Breathe to connect your body to your brain and slow down the triggered spin.
3. Sit down. This will ground you and get some of your spinning-head energy calmed.
4. Take a break. "I am taking a time out. I'll be back in 10 minutes after I walk around the block. Thanks." Letting the other person know when you will be back is the respectful thing to do.
5. If your reactions chronically include abusive language or behavior, an anger management program is strongly advised.
6. Take responsibility for your regression, flip-out or inappropriate behavior or anything you said that was hurtful and apologize. "I'm sorry I flipped out. I'd like to talk about what we could do for next time."
7. Identify your sensitive issues. Let those closest to you know about your tender spots. Are you easily triggered when you feel treated like a kid, feel invaded or controlled, feel stupid, feel unappreciated or unacknowledged or feel neglected? Even though those who really care for you will be gentle around your tender spots (when they remember), ultimately, it is your responsibility to attend to your emotional needs.

### When Another Becomes Triggered

1. Listen while telling yourself, "Looks like she is triggered. This is about her, not me." Repeatedly nod your head. When there's a space, indicate that you are listening. When it makes no or little sense, say, "I don't understand. Please tell me another way." Watch for calm.
2. Invite the other person to sit down.
3. When the other person has calmed, have a discussion about what the rant was really about. Make an invitation to hear the story of the disturbing event that happened years ago that was triggered.

4. Discuss a strategy for next time. Sometimes, having a signal like, "Are you feeling triggered?" can help. This absolutely has to be a mutual decision otherwise people feel belittled and the rant is fueled.

## When Both of You Become Triggered

This is like two toddlers in a sandbox throwing pails and dirt at each other with no grown-up supervising. The person with the least amount of out-of-control energy has the best ability to get the two of you out of the pit. Is that a daunting thought? Hopefully, that person is you, the one reading this book. If you can do something different to break the escalation, you can shift the pattern.

1. Do something stupidly funny like throwing yourself on the floor. At least then you'll be grounded.
2. Say something unexpected such as, "What can I do to help?"
3. Suggest a "time out."

## Preventive Measures

1. Put a plan in place.
2. Make appointments to discuss sensitive issues at a convenient time for both of you.
3. Sit. If it's an intimate relationship, hold hands. Then you'll have a barometer of physical tension.
4. Have a signal and agreement for "time outs."
5. Own your problems without blaming others. State, "I have a problem and I ask for your help with it."
6. Express appreciation whenever possible.
7. Acknowledge and celebrate when you have had constructive and healthy interactions.

Research from a book called *High Conflict People in Legal Disputes*, by Bill Eddy, states some interesting facts: 25 million North Americans have a mental disorder of which most of them are unaware. Another 30 million people have traits or tendencies of mental disorders. We can then conclude that between 70 to 80 percent of people can generally handle themselves in a reasonable manner most of the time. Even those of us in the 70 to 80 percentiles can behave unreasonably when under extreme distress. Usually, our co-workers understand those temporary circumstances and eventually we bounce back.

However, it is useful to be aware when we are dealing with those who are in the extreme realms of dysfunction. Their thinking is very rigid with all-or-nothing, black-or-white thinking and an excessive dose of finger pointing. When you decide you are dealing with a mentally disturbed individual, remember:

- Their behavior is unconscious.
- Tell yourself, "This is about him/her."
- Detach yourself emotionally, if you can.
- Use empathy. Listen without getting hooked.
- Calmly educate the out-of-control person about the consequences of his/her thinking and actions.
- Speak and act as respectfully as possible.
- If appropriate, express concern to your employer.
- If you believe the individual is going to do harm to themselves or others, inform your employer. If necessary, call the police.
- Consider no further contact with that person.

## 4. Ease Conflict

WHEN I worked for the *Contemporary Woman* project, the topic of Conflict Resolution was included in the curriculum. My facilitator colleagues smiled as I truly provided the model of a woman who felt terror at the thought of conflicted situations and was working to better stand my ground. It gave the participants comfort and hope while giving me an opportunity to practice creating win-win situations. My co-facilitators were seasoned WOW-Empowered women. Pamela is now a Human Rights Educator with the Alberta Civil Liberties Research Centre and Martha eventually acquired a Masters Degree in Peace, training with the likes of Jimmy Carter. I learned much from these incredible women.

*"When I'm okay and you're okay, we work it out."*

When I hear that two people who spend significant amounts of time with one another—whether in intimate or work-related relationships—never disagree, I wonder who is not speaking up and has become invisible. Conflict is inevitable and a basically healthy aspect of most relationships. Bullying expert, Barbara Coloroso, differentiates between healthy conflict and deliberate, abusive behavior where power is unequal and certain people or populations are targeted. Conflict resolution is dependent on two willing individuals.

Sixteen survey respondents described conflict with co-workers, ten employees with managers and ten managers in relation to their position. Add to that 29 respondents struggling with clients' behaviors plus those who reported struggling with divorce, workplace criticism and micro-managing, and we end up with a huge number of the Woes having elements of conflict.

Comments about co-worker conflict include:

- Negativity in the workplace.
- Argue with co-workers or not talking to them at all.
- Gossip in the workplace. Passive-aggressive behavior.
- General backstabbing.
- Being ignored when new.
- Unfriendly colleagues.
- Snob nurses.
- Carrying all the workload when three people should share.
- Co-workers didn't do their job and expected me to do my work and theirs.
- Mistrust among colleagues.

Examples of employees in conflict with their managers:

- A manager with a 'split personality'…working in Mental Health—unbearable.
- Being overlooked for a promotion twice.
- Working with a difficult boss.
- A supervisor not allowing Christmas off. It was my time off but she would not change the schedule. I asked her why she booked me and she said that she could do whatever she wanted.
- Boss stealing my ideas and passing them off as her own.
- Arrogant, conceited boss.

Managers experience conflict too, and describe it as their most significant workplace challenge:

- Six month nurse strike when I was manager.
- Not being taken seriously as a manger because of my young age.

• Managing staff in a team work setting.
• Jealousy—I became a supervisor and one staff felt she should have gotten the job. Is a very negative person and never saw the positive.
• Inappropriate behavior by an employee with client and I felt responsible.
• Being undermined in my authority.
• Managing a company while on strike, crossing picket-line daily for ten months.

When conflict raises its head, you have four choices in deciding how to handle it:

1. You can avoid it and pretend it does not exist.
2. You can argue, fight or use power plays until someone *wins*.
3. You can leave.
4. You can work to resolve it.

From settling wars of sibling squabbling to Middle East countries or office disagreements, negotiating solutions takes honesty and willingness on both sides. While it takes all parties to agree to a solution, it takes only one to ruin it. Consequently, there are no guarantees of resolution. However, the potential result of reduced stress, fear and unpleasant surprise plus peace, harmony and improved connection makes resolving conflict well worth the effort.

## 5. Plan for Resolution

B EFORE meeting with the person/s with whom you are in conflict, think hard about what your and their needs might be. Behind all the emotion, the tension, the words, the lack of words, the facial expressions and the angst is a genuine emotional, physical or relational need. Yes, some managers may have an emotional need to be in control, to look or feel important, or to be perceived as superior or winning. Think of ways to reframe your experience in a positive way. For example, you might reframe *needs to be in control* to *needs to act responsibility*. Negotiating needs will more effectively move your conversation forward. Begin by arranging a convenient time for all involved to meet.

*"We can both make it better."*

- **Step 1:**
  - Establish some *ground rules*:
    - Sit.
    - Speak, respectfully and truthfully using sentences beginning with *I*.
    - Don't interrupt, yell, name call, blame or shame.

- **Step 2:**
  - Clearly describe the conflict. Example: "When I saw Sue move into a window office, I felt frustrated."

- **Step 3:**
  - Provide the reasons for your position. Example: "I have worked here longer than Sue, have more business visitors and get headaches without natural light."

- **Step 4:**
  - Listen. Listen to identify areas of agreement and disagreement. Check for clarity in understanding.

- **Step 5:**
  - Generate optional solutions. Step back from the issues and identify the underlying needs, interests, assumptions and beliefs.
  - *Brainstorm* solutions, listing as many options as possible.
  - Make a specific and *behavioral agreement*. "It is agreed that I have use of the boardroom for business meetings, will be at the top of the list for the next window office and will arrange for alternate light in my present office." If appropriate, write the agreement down and sign it. Agree to action items being done by whom and when.

- **Step 6:**
  - Agree to *follow up* at a specific time. Check whether the solution is working.
  - The solution should not be *carved in stone*. The agreement may need to be renegotiated.

## Ten Tips for Negotiating

*"We can work this out."*

1. Set a time limit.
2. Agree to a topic or concern. Then stay focused.
3. Be aware of your own biases and triggers.
4. Listen and listen some more. "Seek first to understand, then to be understood."
5. Make your own needs crystal clear with *I* messages while being open to how your needs might be met.
6. Make the environment as safe as possible.
7. If and when strong feelings surface for you, take a time out.
8. If strong feelings come up for others, up your listening.
9. If appropriate, ease the tension with humor.
10. Acknowledge and celebrate cooperation!

### Do Not Email Conflict

Have you ever been involved in an email message bush fire? It starts with one person feeling hurt, dismissed or angry about an email communication. The recipient reacts with a one-up slamming or defensive message. Here is a hypothetical example: Jane writes a message which she unintentionally sends to Sam's inbox. Jane types, "I am deeply offended by Sam's allegation that I mismanaged our organization's funds. Sam should be more concerned with his own lack of meeting attendance." Sam types his message and hits *Reply all.* "Who does Jane think she is?" etc.

This kind of communication is often copied and sent to one, numerous and sometimes massive databanks of other individuals. Sometimes, the offensive communication arrives in the mailboxes of people who have little or no connection to the players or organization. The miscommunication, dysfunction and tension becomes out of control.

Although email is often a more convenient way to transfer data than using a phone, there are disadvantages when conflict is involved. Clicking *Send* is often an automatic response. Words alone convey a small percent of our message. Tone, pace and volume of voice, which the phone offers, increases our understanding. The best situation is when we are in person and can better receive the full message through words, tone, facial and body expression. Facts and information work well with emails. Emails are invaluable for the transfer of data. However, be wary of dealing with relationship dynamics through the Internet.

Some organizations have a policy that any personal or group conflict is to be dealt with at face-to-face meetings. If ever you receive an email with angry, attacking or defensive content, either delete it and don't get involved or, if you are a main player, pick up the phone and arrange to meet with other party. As Voltaire said, "The road to the heart is the ear." Our eyes add understanding. When relationships count, give it your communication all.

## 6. Filter Criticism: Offer Feedback

WORKING with critical management can result in walking away feeling crushed, ruined, cut off at the knees, humbled, humiliated or plain cheesed off. Some professional development experts stand totally against using any form of criticism and then there are the critical hardliners who say, "A manager needs to tell you the naked truth." Some people have been so wounded in their youth by constant putdowns, sarcasm and criticism that they do exactly the same to others or go to the other extreme of never uttering a word of disagreement. Some people seem to be gifted with a critical mind and perspective. Their gift to the world is a logical critique that forewarns of problems. But where is the balance?

Communication expert, Shelle Rose Charvet, wrote:

*Your fine mind can decide what to take in and what to reject. "Cancel! Cancel!"*

Creating and maintaining a positive emotional state is key to performance…Those who learn new skills the quickest and easiest are those who immediately incorporate feedback and suggestions, without justifying what they were doing and without feeling criticized or getting themselves into a bad state.

Dr. Sidney Simon's classic book, *Negative Criticism*, provides a filter or series of questions to ask before we criticize another. Ask yourself:

1. Is this the right time?
2. Can he or she do anything about the situation or behavior?

## Ten Tips on Receiving Criticism

*"Thank you, thank you for your opinion."*

1. Take a breath, stand back emotionally and put the message you just received through Simon's filtering questions. Then ask yourself realistically if it was fair and accurate information.
2. Discern if the message was abusive or helpful, perhaps courageously given (because someone cares about you) information.
3. If you decide it is verbal abuse, say, "STOP!" and walk away. Note: verbal abuse often involves, "You are…" messages, name calling and put downs.
4. Acknowledge receipt of the message with a simple statement, "Thank you for the information."
5. Support yourself with caring self-talk. Tell yourself, "This information is their opinion. I will listen. I don't have to agree. Their opinion may help me in the long run. I get to decide whether to accept their perspective or not. It is okay for me to make mistakes and learn from them."
6. Agree to any part of the criticism that is true and accurate. Do not acknowledge the parts that are off. "Yes, I am late. I am late by five minutes."
7. Learn to say, "I will think it over," rather than making a quick decision to make a change.
8. Apologize if you were in error, insensitive or caused harm.
9. Avoid defending yourself, counterattacking or adding your own self-critical comments.
10. Later, if appropriate, return to the criticism deliverers and tell them if their information was helpful or not.

3. Has he or she heard this before? Is this new information?
4. Am I sure that none of my own hang-ups are involved?
5. Is it possible that this person needs encouragement more than anything else?

After you get through the Simon filter, discern if an employee or colleague would benefit from suggestions for improvement. If *yes*, present it in the form of feedback. Simply say, "I have suggestions for next time." Keep the directives to three or less.

There are some basic differences between criticism and feedback. It is useful to be able to discern between the two:

- **Criticism**:
  - feels like a personal attack with a tone of judgment
  - is, most often, not requested
  - can over-power a person
  - focuses on mistakes rather than learning from mistakes

- **Feedback**:
  - focuses on a specific circumstance or behavior
  - is directed at the problem, not the person
  - can help the situation when it explains and does not judge
  - is supportive observation, information or advice when it considers everyone's feelings
  - is well timed, planned and is shared in a safe and appropriate setting

### Three Ways to Offer Feedback

1. **Acknowledge**
   - Express appreciation for what was said or done that supported or helped you.
     *Example*: "I appreciate your support. Thank you for telling me you agree."
   - Describe any helpful or notable strengths, skills or attitudes.
     *Example*: "I like your ability to stay calm when I'm feeling so frustrated."

2. **Request Change**
   - The three-step process below comes from Shelle Rose Charvet:
     • Make a suggestion.
     *Suggestion*: "I suggest when you make changes to the document that you highlight them."
     • Give two reasons for the suggestion:
        – What it will accomplish (the benefit).
     *Benefit reason*: "Then the team will be alerted to the change and will be able to back you."
        – What it will solve (or prevent).
     *Preventive reason*: "It will also prevent miscommunication."

- Make an encouraging statement.

  *Encouraging statement*: "Your knowledge on this subject has really helped our team make wise decisions."

3. **Sandwich Technique**

The Sandwich Technique has been used extensively by those in management positions and by Toastmasters International as a speech evaluation process. However, it is recommended that this process be used only intermittently. Otherwise, the receiver may automatically brace to hear suggestions for improvement or criticism when actually all that was said were words of acknowledgment. Here are some steps to assist:

- *Begin with your intention to assist and solicit agreement.* "I want to give you some feedback on your presentation performance to help you for next time. Are you interested in my observations and suggestions?"
- *Describe one, two or three areas of strength.* "I noticed your enthusiasm, how you made three clear points and involved the audience."
- *If appropriate, offer one suggestion for improvement (not a criticism).* "Next time you might want to make longer eye contact with your audience."
- *End with a compliment or appreciation.* "I like your commitment to learning."

## 7. Manage Management

Survey respondents made it clear that incompetent, micromanaging, critical or abusive management styles create the most workplace stress. However, it's not uncommon to hear resilient women say, "I've learned to manage my manager."

*"When I feel inadequate, my focus, thinking and competence deteriorate."*

All the strategies in this book, from listening to creating clear boundaries, can assist you in *managing your boss*. But choose them wisely. Observe your manager first. Ask yourself, "What is the problem?" It could be that your boss has poor communication skills, has a fear of losing power and control or is indecisive. It may also help to ask yourself, "What is my manager's emotional need?" Those emotional needs may include to feel in control, to feel important, to feel safe, to feel deserving or to feel special. This shift in perception may help you develop some understanding, if not empathy, for your boss. Here are some suggestions for dealing with a range of tensions created by ineffective bosses:

1. When a manager lacks leadership skills: Make specific suggestions. Example: "I'd like to close the McGregor file. Do I have a *yes* from you?" When he or she is vague with expectations, ask for clarification.
2. When a manager shows insecurity: Express appreciation. Acknowledge his or her efforts.
3. When a manager overloads your In Basket: Ask what his or her priorities are. Ask for advice on how to handle the load in the expected time frame.
4. When a manager does not keep you informed: Request regular meetings. Share your most recent accomplishments and your career aspirations. Ask about any organizational developments. Ask if the company would benefit from you doing more of a certain behavior, doing less of something or doing something differently. You can always ask, "Are there any questions I could ask to improve my performance and/or my relationship with you?" Take an interest in your manager, his or her family, hobbies and career aspirations. Oftentimes, the position and the responsibilities of being a manager leave them feeling isolated. Be on his or her side whenever possible. He or she often needs an ally.

Since you are reading this book, you have proven you're a go-getter with a desire to strengthen your resilience and performance. Hence, one day, if you so choose, you will probably be offered a management or supervisory position. Perhaps you are already in a management position. Even better. At a minimum, your interactions with and observations of management can provide valuable information of how you want, and don't want, to function. Learn from your observations. A survey recipient and Health Educator who was reprimanded in the hospital lobby for attending an educational session described her learning as "how not to manage people." She said, "When I moved into a managerial position, I always remembered this experience." Others reported their learnings as:

- What not to do with colleagues, peers and managers.
- Appreciate all the people who have worked for me and thank them all the time.
- Appreciate a good boss.

## Ten Tips for Managing Micromanagement

*"Excuse me! You're breath is fogging my computer monitor."*

1. Prove you're capable by requesting total control over small tasks. Then do an excellent job to increase your boss' trust.
2. Do a reality check with yourself or a confidant (a peer, company Ombuds, Occupational Health or HR department). Are you inviting over-supervision? Do you take initiative or do you look for direction for even the smallest tasks?
3. Volunteer to do a task that showcases your skills and strengths.
4. Make an assertive statement such as, "I'm confident that I can do this job independently. I will let you know when it is complete."
5. Keep a record of when you are interrupted with unnecessary direction. Log the date, time, topic, length of conversation and what was said.
6. Request a meeting with your manager or supervisor and express your concerns. Explain how you feel and state what would be helpful. Keep to the facts. Speak with an attitude of, "I have a problem and I want your help."
7. Avoid sentences that begin with *you*. Begin your comments with I. "I feel incompetent when I don't have some freedom doing my job." "I like tackling jobs and running with them."
8. Ask clarifying questions. "What do I need to do so you will trust my work?" "What exactly are my job responsibilities?"
9. If you don't make progress with your manager, go to the supervisor or senior management to see if anything can be done.
10. If, after significant effort, change doesn't happen, you still feel disrespected and your morale is still sinking, request a transfer to another department and/or begin a job search. You deserve better.

Micromanagement is a cluster of behaviors used by managers who closely observe and/or attempt to control the work of their employees. Instead of giving general instructions for small tasks and supervising larger concerns, the micromanager oversees and assesses every step. The result tends to be employees feeling unappreciated and incompetent. This usually leads to employees developing a dislike for their boss.

Don Lowman, a Canadian management and human resources consultant with Towers Perrin, said in a study report, "What we're hearing is that people want to contribute. But they say their leaders and supervisors unintentionally put obstacles in their path." The same study concluded that only 17 percent of Canadians are *highly engaged*, that is willing to devote extra effort to work. Micromanaging clearly contributes to disengagement. Thomas Ng of the University of Hong Kong reported that an employee's sense of control over their work is crucial for motivation. Regardless of the statistics, being micromanaged is a disempowering experience. As one survey respondent wrote, "It sucks!"

If you are doing your job and your manager is still acting like *big brother*, you are being micromanaged. No one likes others peering over their shoulder and snooping into their desk drawers. It becomes problematic when you develop stress symptoms and feel lethargic, fearful, frustrated and depressed. The result is minimized productivity, suppressed or explosive feelings, self-doubt and, ultimately, sick leave or dismissal.

# IV
## Take WOW Action: You Can Do It!

> *Ready, aim and fire. Take action that will bring pride in your self and renewed calm.*

- Champion Change
- Acknowledge and Demonstrate Your Strengths
- *Make Up Your Mind*, Decide
- Demonstrate Courage
- Go Back to School, *Maybe*
- Be Laid Off without Laying Down
- Quit or Resign

## 1. Champion Change

W

HEN we choose change, we often feel excited and exhilarated, and sometimes wonder if we are out of our minds. When change is thrust upon us, we often feel cheated, betrayed and lost. Some of my major personal and forced adjustments include the death of loved ones, needing to sell and leave a beautiful home, being laid off from the *Contemporary Woman* project and the loss of perceiving myself as a caring, competent and loving mother.

> *Change is inevitable but handling it well isn't.*

Flexibility is required to thrive, especially during times of accelerated change. Brooks and Goldstein, in their book, *The Power of Resilience*, support the power of the Serenity Prayer. They confirm that when we accept what we *can't change* and take ownership of what we *can change*, we feel better empowered. I cherish fond memories of my dear ones who died. That beautiful home belongs to another family and we learned to love wherever we rest our head at night. My work has transformed into a bigger picture of empowering women, and men too. I'm back to perceiving myself as not only a caring mother but a loving woman of many people.

In 1962, Ohio State University professor, Everett Rogers, coined the phrase *innovators, early adopters, early majority and laggards.* Indeed, people vary from feeling thrilled to being terrified in their attitude and response to change. Of course, reactions vary depending on the circumstances. Note which of the following five categories typically describes you:

1. **The Innovator**: "I have ideas about changing this challenge into an opportunity. I can hardly wait."
2. **The Quick Adapter**: "Great idea. How can I help?"
3. **The Doubter**: "I'm not sure. You'll have to prove it to me."
4. **The Resister**: "What's wrong with the way we've always done it?"
5. **The No Wayer**: "It will never work. I will kick and scream to take us back to *the good old days.*"

To influence others' attitudes and behaviors, we need to offer people fewer logical reasons for change and offer more emotional reasons for change. In *The Heart of*

## Ten Tips for Opening up to Change

*"I've done hard before and I can again."*

1. Do a risk analysis. Ask, "What do I have to gain and/or lose from this change?"
2. Every now and then, take a calculated risk just for the sheer joy of it. You might bungee jump, visit a nudist beach or try street performing with your saxophone.
3. Take a risk in the name of self-care.
4. When you initiate change for yourself, whether it's seeking new friends or starting an exercise program, expect setbacks and be prepared with alternate plans.
5. Take a small step toward a long-held dream.
6. Say *no* to activities you find meaningless.
7. Make a list of what you want To Be (more creative), To Do (work less with paper and more with people) and To Have (my own office).
8. Notice when you whine or grumble.
9. Identify what you could do to satisfy the grump within.
10. When disagreeable change is forced upon you, use the Serenity Prayer for support: "God, grant me the serenity to accept the things I cannot change, the courage to change the things I can, and the wisdom to know the difference."

*Change*, John Kotter writes, "Both thinking and feeling are essential and both are found in successful organizations, but the heart of change is in the emotions."

## 2. Acknowledge and Demonstrate Your Strengths

FROM the time WOW-Empowered Faye McGhee discovered her strengths of observation, compassion and encouragement as a teacher's aide, she has continued to refine her skills. Faye had the advantage of clarity in her strengths. But what if you don't? A nurse and survey respondent admitted, "I was in the wrong job for my skill set and personality and wouldn't admit it then." Four other respondents described being fired because their jobs were "not a good fit."

Help is available. Often times, the strength you admire in others can provide a clue. Additional information comes from research studies on the subject. When the Gallup

Poll asked, "What percentage of a typical day do you spend playing to your strengths?" a disappointing 17 percent of the respondents reported "most of the time." Martin Seligman, Christopher Peterson and Marcus Buckingham have become leaders in the *Use Your Strengths* movement. Following in the footsteps of personality inventories such as the Myers Briggs Indicator, the Clifton Strengths-Finder and Seligman's Signature Strengths are quizzes that help you determine your key strengths. You can access Buckingham's inventory through his books and Seligman's at <**http:// www.authentichappiness.sas. upenn.edu/Default.aspx**>.

*"My mother told me to stop talking so much. Now they pay me to do it."*

When I answered the 240 questions on the Authentic Happiness website, my number one strength came up as Creativity while my second strength was Teamwork. Yeah! I feel affirmed that I am joyfully using my strengths.

For our purposes, the definition of strengths is a combination of three factors: 1. innate **talent**, such as thinking logically, 2. **skill**, such as how to use the logic to design a bridge, and 3. **knowledge**, such as an understanding of the materials and necessary structure to complete the task. All strengths can be developed. However, when you have strong inherent **talents**, the accompanying tasks are more easily accomplished. For example, if you are like me, you expend a great deal of energy and effort thinking logically and with detachment. If given the choice, thinking more randomly and creatively comes with ease. You can learn the **skill** of writing a logical pro and con decision list and access the **knowledge** needed to decide which item goes on the pro or con side. Yet, for the creative intuitive person, this process requires more exertion.

Your actions and the resulting successes demonstrate your strengths to others. When people demonstrate creativity, they feel excited about change and challenge, they think of new solutions, and they imagine a successful end result. We all know people who are stuck in the *same old*, who say "but we've always done it that way" and resist change. Creativity is not their strength but orderliness may be. A picture of my office would indicate that creativity is one of my major strengths while I would benefit from the services of a professional organizer. All weaknesses can be improved yet we blossom when we build on our natural strengths. As Seligman says, "Building strength and virtue is not about learning, training or conditioning, but about discovery, creation and ownership." Begin by identifying your strengths.

## Name Your Strengths

| | | | | |
|---|---|---|---|---|
| Acceptance | Detachment | Honesty | Methodical | Playfulness |
| Adaptability | Discernment | Independence | Modesty | Practicality |
| Analytical Thinking | Discipline | Inclusiveness | Motivation | Purposefulness |
| Assertiveness | Empathy | Innovation | Objectiveness | Reliability |
| Cooperativeness | Enthusiasm | Intuition | Observance | Respectfulness |
| Courage | Emotional Smarts | Kindness | Optimism | Responsibility |
| Courtesy | Esthetic Smarts | Leadership Ability | Orderliness | Service Orientation |
| Creativity | Forgiveness | Logic | Passion | Social Smarts |
| Curiosity | Generosity | Love of Learning | Patience | Trustworthiness |
| Decisiveness | Gratefulness | Love | Persistence | Other? |

Intuitively knowing that she could burn out using her strengths, Faye McGhee, developed a moderating stance. She said, "Just because I am skilled enough, gifted with a talent or have the knowledge base for a needed project or task, it does not mean it is me who has to do it." I concur.

For years, I would extend myself based on co-worker's compliments. First, I would be told, "Oh Patricia! You are so enthusiastic and creative!" "Yup," I'd agree. I had just demonstrated those two strengths. Then, almost immediately, I would agree to another task, sometimes out of my strength zone. Knowing your strengths doesn't mean you have to be sucked into using them indiscriminately. In actuality, if a strength is used too often in the wrong place or with the wrong people, it could be labeled a *weakness*. Take charge. Enjoy using your strengths and notice your improved work satisfaction.

### 3. *Make Up Your Mind*, **Decide**

ONE thing is certain: we are bombarded daily with myriad choices and are subsequently called to make hundreds of decisions. Most of our personal decisions seem inconsequential. After all, does it really matter what you eat for breakfast? It might. Decisions repeatedly acted upon become habits. Habits form your life structure. If your breakfast regularly consists of food that is high in fat and loaded with sugar, you could, over time, put yourself at risk for obesity, diabetes or heart failure. Changing habits requires firm resolutions.

*since not deciding is deciding, decisively decide to decide.*

The late Psychotherapist and Plastic Surgeon, Dr. Maxwell Maltz, noted that it takes 21 days to create a new habit. The 21 Day Habit Theory is now an accepted premise for concerted behavior change. And, it may take longer. The more important the result or outcome of a decision, the more thought and consideration is warranted. Years ago, after being rejected for a job facilitating women's groups for the *Contemporary Woman* project, I discussed the situation with my support group. With their encouragement, I called back the primary interviewer to gather information.

Sometimes you need to ask some hard questions even though you may not like the answers. I asked her to tell me what she perceived as my weaknesses and what suggestions she had for improvement. It was hard and valuable to learn that my answers rambled and were vague. She added, "We require a role model of clarity and assertiveness for these women." Indeed, I had a habit of filling air space for the sake of avoiding silence and giving little thought before speaking. I decided to develop a new habit of containing my answers and communicating with clarity. Two years later, I applied again and was chosen.

From that experience, I learned two important lessons:

1. For major decisions, it is important to consult with others for a different and objective perspective. Ask at least three wise people, "What would you do if you were me?" They can brainstorm options, ask clarifying questions and help you identify the advantages and disadvantages of each alternative. They can also hold you accountable to take action. However, remember that your decision needs to be *your* responsibility. Please avoid leaning on others to make decisions for you.

## Ten Tips for Decision Making

*"Like my bed, I've made up my mind and it's looking good."*

1. Define the problem or opportunity.
2. Collect pertinent information.
3. Brainstorm a list of options with your support people. Seven or more is recommended.
4. Narrow the list by choosing the options aligned with your values.
5. Narrow the list to two or three options by considering the advantages and disadvantages.
6. Notice your gut reaction.
7. Make your decision.
8. Decide when and where to take action.
9. Take action.
10. Evaluate.

2. Undesirable habits *can* be changed. Identify the problem, take ownership, look for solutions, put a plan in place and take action.

### Up-Against-a-Deadline Decision

When under pressure, we are more apt to make a decision that results in unnecessary pain, wasted time and uncalled-for expense. Being emotionally prepared for potentially time-sensitive decisions helps.

## Ten Tips for Pressured & Time-Sensitive Decisions

*"Get crackin', and I'm not talking egg-istentially."*

1. If you can foresee a potentially damaging situation, create a back up plan.
2. Have a clear job description and know your organization's policies and guidelines.
3. Breathe. Feel your feet. Calm yourself. Use your head and heart.
4. Imagine a very wise person. Ask, "What would 'Lois' do in this situation?"
5. Believe, "It's okay to make the best choice possible with the available information."
6. Take action.
7. Accept that mistakes happen.
8. Take responsibility for your part.
9. Learn how you can make a better decision next time.
10. Consider saying, "I need more time to make a smart decision."

## 4. Demonstrate Courage

ALL the women who contributed to this book have demonstrated courage in some form or other. Bravery is a prerequisite of resilience; to be able to bounce back from adversity and face what may initially feel overwhelming. It's easy to see resilience in our esteemed role models—in Mother Teresa and her work with the poor in the slums of Calcutta; Margaret Sanger, who received a prison sentence because of her pioneering efforts to educate women living in the ghettoes of New York City about contraception; Oprah Winfrey, who rose to success after a challenging childhood that included poverty and sexual abuse. The danger is to compare ourselves and conclude we have never done an act of courage. Not so! As Arianna Huffington wrote in *On Becoming Fearless…In Love, Work, and Life*, "Fearlessness is not the absence of fear. It's the mastery of fear. It's about getting up one more time than we fall down."

## Ten Tips to Feel the Fear & Do Your Work Anyway

*"I can keep myself safe."*

1. Support yourself when feeling anxious and still take justified action.
2. Flex your courage. Take a risk outside your comfort zone. You might challenge a procedure that others protect with "we've always done it that way." You might ask for a raise or an extended benefits package.
3. Exercise and become physically strong.
4. Take an assertiveness or self-defense class.
5. If you lived in fear as a child, tell yourself that, as an adult, you can now take care of yourself.
6. Edit out disempowering thoughts.
7. If you have an irrational fear or phobia, arrange for therapy. Phobias typically are easily diminished.
8. Think of all the times you have demonstrated courage.
9. Choose a courageous role model.
10. Become your own hero.

Some days it takes all the courage you can muster to get up in the morning and face deadlines, disempowering management, disgruntled co-workers, dissatisfied clients or the myriad other workplace challenges you'd just as soon toss in the rubbish bin. However, facing them is an act of courage. Acknowledge and applaud your everyday acts of courage.

If you often feel frail, intimidated, scared, anxious or powerless and the idea of demonstrating courage is daunting, consider taking assertiveness or self-defense training. When I signed on for a month-long work-study program at the California, human potential retreat, Esalen, I was assigned to a learning group under the guidance of Robert Nadeau. Nadeau is one of the first Americans to train in Japan as an Aikido master or Sensei. I initially thought we were going to learn meditation and grounding techniques but our experience with Nadeau was much richer. He helped us trust our *body truth* and personal power. We threw pillows at one another, like soft attacks, learning to receive the thrust and spin the energy force easily yet powerfully back at our opponent. We learned to ground our bodies, flow with mock attacks, stay balanced and in charge of *our space*.

When I returned home, I felt mentally, emotionally and physically stronger than when I left. I was also better equipped to demonstrate courage. My fear of in-home counseling in some high-risk neighborhoods was realistically minimized—minimized to the point that I knew I could feel the fear and take action to take care of myself. Not only did I put in place appropriate protective factors, I knew I could call upon my ability to hold *my space*.

Take time for courage—courage to seek the job you really want, courage to take time for yourself, courage to stop doing what doesn't work for you and courage to stand up to the world's injustices. Ask yourself songwriter Jana Stanfield's question, "What would I do today if I were brave?"

## 5. Go Back to School, *Maybe*

Your present work may be rewarding and satisfying, or not. When you look at your work hours, what percentage flies by when you are in the zone and when you have a sense of a *job well done*? Fedora's factory job was 10 to 15 percent satisfactory—it paid the bills. Her hair styling career, however, gets an 80 percent. Decide what percentage is acceptable for you. What is your bottom line percentage? Even in my present occupation as an author, therapist and professional speaker, there are a number of activities, usually paper work, which are challenging for me to complete. Fortunately, most of my work has been and continues to be more than satisfactory. For example, I garnered about 85 percent satisfaction from my work as facilitator of the 14-week, *Contemporary Woman* project.

*Real education comes in many forms. Discover yours.*

If your satisfaction rate is less than your acceptable bottom line, you need to consider changing jobs or go back to school. Do anything except stay in an unfulfilling work situation. In the *Contemporary Woman* project, I worked with women who temporarily and financially were supported by social assistance or employment insurance (EI). They needed to target and attain satisfying employment. The process included matching their skills and passions to meaningful employment opportunities. Work placements were arranged to give participants a taste of a prospective career path. It didn't matter if it was scrubbing dogs in a doggie wash or shadowing an accountant in a busy office during tax season, the fit showed immediately. It showed in the women's faces, eyes, posture and language. If the job was a poor fit, the women were left feeling discouraged, lost and frustrated. They needed to again begin the process of researching, evaluating and trying on a new future career. If our initial research was a fit, however, the women beamed, their lips hurt from smiling and they walked with a lilt. They were excited at the prospect of leaping into the required training and education.

For some of the participants, the idea of going back to school was not welcomed. They often had nasty childhood memories of the classroom. Please note that returning to school is not always necessary to reach career goals. Famous school drops outs include Oscar-winning actress and singer, Julie Andrews, British author, Jane Austen, Canadian super singer, Anne Murray, and multi-millionaire and renegade marketer, Christine Comaford-Lynch. However, as exemplified by these exceptionally successful individuals, continual learning (even if it is not in a classroom) is always mandatory.

Just as Fedora identified her natural skills—hand-eye coordination, creativity, ability to communicate, attention to detail—identifying strengths is an essential component for choosing a new career direction. Interviews, questionnaires and inventories such as the Strong Campbell and the Myers-Briggs Indicator can be arranged through community colleges, universities or career counselors. Barbara Sher has made it her business to help people find their dream jobs. One of her awareness exercises is to write out a description of a workday in heaven and another in hell. She also suggests recalling what people told you as a child would be a good fit for you. Did your Mom ever say, "Oh, you argue so logically you could be a lawyer." Mom, Dad and Grandma usually identify abilities long before school counselors and human resource personnel do.

An excellent search strategy is to find someone doing what you imagine is your dream job. These people are usually more than willing to share the challenges and rewards of their job. Our son, Ben, is an animal lover. Because of him, we had a rotating menagerie of household pets—gerbils, dogs, cats, rabbits and birds. While working in a pet store, he started to dream of owning his own shop. Fortunately, he interviewed the owner and discovered that in order to be successful he would have to be a business person before a pet lover. Ben, now a paramedic, lives with his wife, son and two dogs.

Resigning is not always necessary to find meaningful work. Look for opportunities to train within your present organization. Some companies will subsidize advanced education. Top organizations support continual employee learning. You have nothing to lose by asking and much to gain. Few jobs are 100 percent fulfilling. But you deserve a number over 75 percent.

## 6. Be Laid Off without Laying Down

BEING let go from a workplace can be a traumatic experience, an opportunity, or both. I have twice been laid off. Each time was when government funding was terminated and we had to close down programs.

*"You're fired!" can shatter our sense of capability and value.*

There were ten family counselors affected by Cambyr Agencies collapse in the 1990s. It was a shock to us all. The director called us together and gave us the news. There were tears. One staff member ran out of the room. Mark listened. He answered questions. He made it clear that he would gladly write us reference letters and support us in our next step. He handled it well, yet most of us needed to grieve before we were able to refocus.

When the *Contemporary Woman* project lost its funding, I was ready to open a private practice and begin speaking professionally. The transition was done with ease. When asked how they responded to being laid off, some survey respondents wrote about their dramatic life improvements. Discoveries included heightened self-awareness, maturity and wisdom. One woman wrote, "I became more cautious in dealing with others and this was beneficial—I was no longer so gullible and naïve." Another wrote, "I discovered and affirmed my strengths and talents." Others realized the job was not a good fit and sought different professions. When they were ready, they found new and exciting opportunities.

Other women were not so optimistic. They had bills to pay, a family to support and no immediate options for employment. In hindsight, they wrote:

- Be prepared with a second detour road.
- Life is unpredictable and you need to decide what's important that excites and sustains you.
- People are always dispensable. Know that and do your best under the circumstances.
- Things could be worse.
- Time moves on and you can learn from the experience.

If you are in the middle of a program closure, downsizing or merger, the following will help you avoid getting down on yourself. When there is talk of downsizing, start planning. If it happens, you will be ready and, if it doesn't happen, you will feel relieved. Here are some considerations:

- Update your resume. It will give you confidence should you have to job search. Describe your accomplishments in numbers where possible. "Effectively supervised a unit of 25 full-time staff for over three years."
- Gather endorsement letters from managers and colleagues whenever possible. Don't wait until you are laid off.
- Sock away some emergency funds now—three months living expenses is recommended.
- Decide what you want to do in the next ten years of your life. Make sure you know what you don't want to do before deciding what you do want to do. Describe a perfect day of work.
- Apply for and go for job interviews while employed. Begin to sniff out exciting and available possibilities. Experiment with positions in which you have little interest. That way, if you are not short-listed, you won't be upset and you will have gained valuable interview experience.

Once the announcement is made:

1. File for employment insurance (EI) immediately. You can cancel later but at least you will have some interim income.
2. Check your wardrobe and practice job interview skills. Get a book on effective interviewing.
3. If you aren't clear about your choice of direction, choose temporary, contract or part-time positions.
4. Consider free-lancing, consulting or entrepreneurship. If you have ever dreamt of a new career, now is the time to make the big leap.

## 7. Quit or Resign

THIRTY-FOUR survey respondents reported that they resigned from their work as their way to cope with their biggest adversity in the workplace. Many tried other strategies first. One wrote that she had a "boss from hell who threw things." She reported, "I tried to change the things I could, work with what I couldn't change and then finally left." Some women regret not walking out the door sooner. One put up with bullying far too long. "After five years, I quit with my resilience barely intact." In response to the question, "How did you cope?" a manager expressed her regret for staying. "I should have left sooner. The environment was poison for me." Some women view resignation

*You can walk out like a mad cow, a scared mouse or a dignified woman.*

as a personal failure as reflected in this disclosure. "I quit and wept in my basement for a month." Others wrote, "Quit and cried," or, "Cried and quit."

Sometimes, resigning is an effective solution and, other times, not. Mary Lou Quinlan cautions in *Time Off for Good Behavior: How Hardworking Women Can Take a Break and Change Their Lives*:

> Quitting your job may feed your need for revenge and provide some immediate sense of relief, but be sure you've thought through your reasons for doing it. Unless you're independently wealthy, your grievances should be very serious, or your plan well thought out....Quitting is a solution I'd never recommend to women who are the sole support of their families, or are barely making it paycheck to paycheck.

Contrary to Quinlan's advice, Carole Kanchier, author of the award winning book, *Dare to Change Your Job and Your Life* writes, "Don't use lack of money as an excuse for not making a career change." She believes women can find ways to survive and thrive through the transition. Fedora, who moved on to be a hairstylist, demonstrated that a plan does minimize the potential risks involved in quitting. Often, as described by survey respondents, you risk your health, intimate relationships and confidence if you stay in a toxic or unrewarding work situation. Life is full of taking risks whether we get out of bed or not. It's up to us to draw the map of where we want to go.

The decision is a very personal one. Women can experience personal empowerment through quitting. They close one door to open another. A corporate administrator who was micro managed and then passed over for a promotion wrote, "I walked away and went to a new opportunity. It made me grow and stick up for myself." Sometimes, we can resign with a smile because an opportunity just too good to pass up comes along. Other times, it is like we are committing mutiny on our comrades in battle by leaving. Here are some ideas on how to leave with grace:

- Seek alternate solutions such as speaking to management or asserting yourself before proceeding with a resignation.
- Ask for letters of reference if possible before moving on.
- Avoid burning bridges if possible.
- Avoid blaming or finger pointing.

- Frame your resignation as a decision to move onto a different or higher-level position.
- If you feel out of integrity because you have not taken action about a workplace injustice, address it before you walk out the door.

# V
## Connect for Added WOW Power

*We all benefit from relationships in which it is safe to share problems, ideas, solutions, laughter and tears.*

- Give and Receive Acknowledgement
- Be a Brazen Gal: Self Promote
- Get a Little Help from Your Friends
- Nurture a Supportive Love Relationship
- Create Your Village
- Give Up Your Grudge
- Seek an Inclusive and Respectful Workplace

# 1. Give and Receive Acknowledgement

WE all crave to be seen, heard and acknowledged. Whether I say that to individuals, groups or large audiences, heads nod in the affirmative. When I first began working in a counseling agency, I was thrilled with the supervision. My manager smiled, nodded and listened as I worked out my problems through non-stop, extroverted talking. As I exited from his office, I would turn, thank him for his time and he would respond with a generous laugh and a big "You're most welcome." I left notes of appreciation on his desk and the occasional homemade muffin. I was surprised, therefore, when I learned that long-time employees felt frustrated by his lack of wise guidance. The lesson? Acknowledgement and a sense of gratitude improve working conditions whether it is sent or received by employees or management.

*Filling people's emotional piggy bank costs nothing, yet can be invaluable.*

"Sawu Bona" is a South African greeting which literally means, "I see you." Its deeper meaning is "because you are there, I exist," that "without each other, we literally do not exist." Imagine what your workplace would be like if this acknowledgement was genuinely sent and received on a daily basis.

Appreciation is undervalued by many organizations while being a key ingredient for a thriving workplace. This is the conclusion from countless management experts and research projects. In *How Full is Your Bucket? Positive Strategies for Work and Life*, Tom Rath and Dr. Donald Clifton said that the main reason most North Americans leave their jobs is that they don't feel appreciated. Their conclusions also include:

- Sixty-five percent of Americans received no recognition at work last year.
- Ninety percent of people say they are more productive when around people with a positive attitude.
- Five positive interactions are needed to counteract one negative interaction.

In *Encouraging the Heart: A Leader's Guide to Rewarding and Recognizing Others*, James Kouzes, Professor of Leadership, and Barry Z. Posner, Dean of the Leavey School of Business at Santa Clara University, describe a fascinating experiment. They asked their leadership class how they would answer the following question. "Do I *need* encouragement to perform at my best?" Sixty percent answered in the affirmative. When

## Ten Tips for Acknowledging

*"I see you. I hear you."*

1. Minimize negative words and phrases such as *can't*, *but*, *no*, *never*, *always*, *should* and *impossible*.
2. Avoid saying *You are* followed by *wrong*, *incompetent*, *at fault* or any blame-throwing words.
3. Remind yourself that most of us are doing the best we can.
4. Listen first to discern what is going on for the other person.
5. Acknowledge feelings. Feelings are never right or wrong.
6. Acknowledge people's best intentions. If you don't know what they intended, assume that their intentions were *to do no harm*.
7. Note and comment on people's accomplishments and strengths.
8. Act as if you are a cheerleader or a supportive coach.
9. Learn to watch and listen with a sense of gratitude.
10. Express appreciation.

they changed the question to, "When you get encouragement, does it help you perform at a higher level?" 98 percent answered yes.

A dissertation from Benedictine University called *Appreciative Inquiry* concluded that workers who felt appreciated by management were 52 percent less likely to look for different employment. Money is an important compensation for work but so are human factors such as being valued. People who feel appreciated tend to have more positive attitudes about work and their contribution to it.

Appreciation has the biggest impact when it is given randomly. B.F. Skinner discovered that random reinforcement more strongly anchors behaviors than consistent reward. Consider how we view bosses who arrange a *surprise* on Administrative Assistants' Day compared to a boss who for no reason acts with a gesture of appreciation. It's similar to gestures of affection in intimate relationships. Compare the romantic scale of a single rose gifted on Valentine's Day with one given on an *ordinary* day.

## Ten Tips to Amply Appreciate

*"Have I told you lately how much I appreciate you?"*

1. Express high expectations about what people are capable of accomplishing.
2. Let others know you have confidence in their abilities.
3. Pay more attention to people's cooperative, helpful and wise acts than their omissions, errors and misjudgments.
4. Tell stories about special achievements of team members.
5. Celebrate group and individual accomplishments.
6. Spend time listening to the needs and interests of other people.
7. Personalize the recognition you give to others.
8. Show others, by your own example, how people should be recognized and rewarded.
9. Recognize people in public for exemplary work.
10. Congratulate people for a job well done with expressions of recognition:
    - I appreciate your effort.
    - Thank you for your time and contribution.
    - I like your eagerness.
    - I see you put in a lot of time working on this.
    - I believe you put a lot into this.

## 2. Be a Brazen Gal: Self Promote

SELF-PROMOTION is the ability to let others know your strengths, capabilities and accomplishments. A study by the employee research and consulting firm, Towers Perrin-ISR, found that, "For women, it's all about what's good for the company. For men, it's more about strategies for advancement." Women tend to feel awkward even when it is appropriate to present themselves in the best possible light. "Silly little me," is often easier for women to say than, "My strengths include…"

As a therapist and woman, my attention was focused on acknowledging others. When I made a career shift into professional speaking, I felt uncomfortable when told I needed to promote and sell myself. If you're like me, your initial reaction might be to judge this whole idea as crass. But we're not talking about in-your-face pushiness or arrogance. We're talking about informing others. Yes, it is often to our advantage but it

## Ten Tips for Blowing Your Own Horn

*"I have exciting news."*

1. Shift from talking about your responsibilities to telling stories about your accomplishments—from, "I have responsibility for my department's data inputting," to, "Last week my manager had a rush job. I was working on another project but I managed to accurately input 5,000 plus words and format the annual report. Wait until you see it!"
2. Use numbers when possible. "I was surprised to realize that I averaged $10,000 in monthly sales for the company last year."
3. Talk with passion about what you have read or learned. "The university class on *Positive Inquiry* gave me many tools that I now use to improve my staff's morale."
4. Offer help to others. "I will gladly forward you my article that shows how to do that."
5. Speak up and volunteer when you hear opportunities to use your strengths. "I can do that! It's similar to a project I did last year."
6. Think of yourself as a helpful sales representative. You are selling your ideas and worth.
7. Find a colleague who will promote you and, in return, do likewise.
8. Make a list of your major achievements.
9. Journal your daily accomplishments.
10. Bring celebrative treats to share when a major task or project is completed.

is also often to other's advantage. Every day, we sell or promote our ideas, proposed actions or positions. I began to think of self-promotion as a way to inform others about solutions I could provide for their challenges. Let's say you had the cure for cancer. Wouldn't you promote your solution? You have experience, information and answers that others don't. By announcing your offerings, your organization, the world, can become a better place.

The other aspect of letting yourself be known is deciding on the image you want to present. You can choose any picture you want from Rock Star to Geek. How you dress, walk, talk and relate gives a message. There are endless choices. Think of a car. What model and make would you be? Would you choose a sensible compact version or a

*That little light of yours, please let it shine!*

sports car? When you buy a new car, you make sure it is shiny and clean. Then you show it off to your friends and family. Whatever illusion or image of yourself you decide to present, do it to the max. We benefit by doing the same with our abilities.

The basic guideline for résumé writing will also help you request a raise or a promotion. It will also assist you in a job interview or when starting your own business. The basic guideline is this—always present the best possible picture of yourself. Self-promotion when done in the service of others takes away from the possibility of arrogant and aggressive pitching. It is true that aggressive promotion is offensive. Just remember the last time you cleverly escaped a pushy sales representative. However, there are ways to blow your own horn and still have people like you.

## 3. Get a Little Help from Your Friends

SOCIAL support is a key resilience factor known to help us regain focus after experiencing difficulty. Bonnie Amundson developed a deep appreciation and use of the strengthening role of different kinds of friendships. She effectively interacted with work friends to provide on the spot support, guidance and appreciation. At the same time she knew that avoiding negative gossip and having clear boundaries including no flirting helps with workplace focus and productivity.

*"I saw my best self in the reflections of my women friends."*

Like-minded people are often attracted to the same kind of career path or profession. The workplace has been where three of my closest friendships were made. And those same friends have supported me through some rough times. I actually calm in their presence. Here's the friendship proof. An exciting theory of stress response for women was reported by Professor Shelley E. Taylor and her team at UCLA. In 1998, they began to wonder if women had different reactions to stress than males. By 2000, they reported a phenomenon they called *Tend and Befriend*.

The *befriend* piece of the research was derived partly from studies in anthropology. Since the cave years, females have grouped together to share caregiving, prepare food and to protect one another. Our pioneer ancestors were still contributing to family survival when they gathered to make quilts or peel enough potatoes to feed the wheat thrashers. Now here's the exciting conclusion and good news. Women, whether at home or in their place of employment, need to gather together. They need each other to share their *herstories*, to *aah* in empathy, to access assistance with demands, and to nurture one another with encouragement. All this supportive give and take helps relieve women's everyday stress.

Yet, many of us have been told to keep our work relationships at arm's length; not to become too friendly with our co-workers. Indeed, researcher, Tom Rath, reports that about one-third of the 80,000 managers and leaders he and the Gallup Poll interviewed, supported the old adage, "Familiarity breeds contempt." While acknowledging the negative consequences of some workplace friendships, Rath enthusiastically encourages the development of a workplace buddy, someone with whom you can congratulate and commiserate. He reports that the over 30 percent of employees who have a best friend at work are seven times more likely to be engaged at work, be more productive, be more engaging with clients, be more innovative and be supported to do their best every day. Rath also discovered, "Employees who have a close friendship with their manager are more than 2.5 times as likely to be satisfied with their job." These findings provide significant support to the theory that social supports provide a key resilience strengthening and protective factor.

### Four Friendship Basics
- Give and take when it comes to calling, supporting, sharing and listening.
- Be willing to receive and kindly tell *hard truths*.
- Develop friendships at work and outside of work with appropriate boundaries for different situations; different friends for different reasons.
- Avoid developing friendships with those who take you for granted, only connect when they want something or have negative or toxic attitudes and behaviors.

### Four Steps for Beginning a Friendship

- **Step 1: Greet**
The first time you meet someone say, "Hi. How are you?" for a playful introduction. "Hello. How do you do you?" can be used for formal situations. It is always appropriate to add, "I'm so glad to meet you." Exchange names with,

"My name is Patricia and your name is?" Use that person's name two or three times to put it in your memory bank—at least for the duration of your initial conversation. Some people balk at the ritual "game." I hear people say, "I don't like to be bothered with small talk." Yet, ritualistic talk provides a safe space to check out mutual interest. Keep asking and answering questions as evenly as possible. If you receive brisk answers with little reciprocation of interest, move on by saying, "It was great chatting with you." If at any time in the conversation the sharing does not feel balanced or politely connected, move on.

### • Step 2: Geography

Places of residence, work, vacation and birth can be safely discussed as long as the two of you are engaged. It's a non-personal, low risk topic. You can talk about geography for up to an hour to fill in time at a corporate event. It sounds like this. "What part of the city do you live in?" "What do you like about your community?" "Where is your favorite holiday spot?" "Why?" By talking about geography, you stay on safe and non-intimate topics while getting a better feel for the other person. Reciprocate with your own geographical information.

### • Step 3: Activities

If you and your companion decide there is an interest in spending future time together, you can introduce the topics of work activities and hobbies. Bouncing back and forth about passions and favorite pastimes can be fun and lively. People's eyes often shine when they talk. "I love going to movies like *Beaches* starring Bette Midler that have great character development and provide not only a great laugh but a good cry." If you find a project or activity with mutual interest, you can begin to develop a relationship.

### • Step 4: Feeling Risk Analysis

Before setting a time and place to share a mutual activity, share a tender feeling to test the emotional safety of your future companion. "Sometimes at the movies, if there is a scary part, and I mean just a little spooky, I feel so nervous I pull my sweater over my head." Now if your conversational partner says, "That's dumb," there's no way you will enjoy going to the movies with this dude or babe. If the response is, "I've thought of doing the same thing myself," you have received a signal to head for the closest movie theatre.

## Mentors

Workplace mentors are worth mentioning here. A mentor, who is typically a step or more ahead of your aspirations, provides wise guidance, instruction and support for significant challenges. Unlike friendships, a mentor does not function as an equal or peer. A mentor is like an informal teacher who helps improve our knowledge, problem-solving skills, and communication or leadership capacity. Your mentor might be your manager, might be someone who works for another organization or may be an inspiring person you met at your professional association.

Mentorship can be informal or formal. You might choose not to tell a mentor that you have chosen him or her but mentally you are alert to what you can learn from this individual. You would indicate appreciation for guidance by saying something such as, "Thank you for the guidance and insight." In a formal situation you both agree to a mentorship relationship and might create lists of desired goals with timelines.

Decide what works best for your situation. Depending on your relationship, you might choose your mother, father, aunt or uncle. Look for someone who is available, listens, has the knowledge and skills you want to acquire, has an interest in your success and is willing to give you both encouraging and room-for-improvement feedback. One day, be open to lending a hand down yourself.

## 4. Nurture a Supportive Love Relationship

THE value of available, supportive and loving arms in marriage is immeasurable. Marriage, as opposed to co-habitation, provides resilience strengthening. British researcher, Nick Powdthavee, surveyed 9,700 married people and 3,300 unmarried people in common-law relationships. He concluded that, if one spouse was basically happy, it helps the other face all kinds of adversity, including unemployment and illness. He also discovered that married people are 30 percent happier and able to cope. Other researchers, such as Maggie Gallagher and Linda J. Waite, claim that marriage changes people for the better with improved health, finances and sexual satisfaction.

For a three-year period, I co-facilitated a marriage preparation program and I still provide some marriage counsel.

It's important to protect your partner from initiation burn out.

## Ten Tips for Couples

*"May we be like two trees sheltering one another from the wind."*

1. Accept your partner's strengths and weaknesses as well as your own strengths and weaknesses. Neither of you are perfect.
2. Realize that what initially attracted you to your partner may be the quality that challenges you the most.
3. Make your relationship a safe place for compassionate truth telling. To that end, listen first and then be heard.
4. Stay committed through the easy and tough times.
5. Be the change you want to see in the relationship.
6. Use words such as *we, our* and *together*.
7. Sprinkle appreciation throughout your day.
8. Beware of coupleship eroders. Don't let children, employment, television, friends and other distractions come between you.
9. Keep in touch. Touch is vital, while lovemaking may ebb and flow.
10. Encourage and celebrate one another.

It's fascinating how some couples walk away after one session grumbling, "It didn't work." That same couple have spent months, often years, digging deep cesspools of resentment and pain. Yet, they expect a therapeutic hour to fix the whole mess without their commitment to make concerted effort for change.

I have a long-term relationship with my hubby, Les. We've been married for over 40 years and as I say, "We still *do it* almost every night of the week—almost on Monday, almost on Tuesday, almost on Wednesday." Seriously though, we have invested in our marital success. We support one another in taking separate holidays because he loves the wilderness and I love educational events and retreats. But we also take mutually satisfying vacations. We've attended couple retreats, workshops and lectures. This year will mark our eighteenth year at the relationship enrichment weekend at the Banff Couples' Conference. We also enjoy adventures that have taken us around the globe.

Marital expert, Dr. John Gottman, claims he can predict with 90 percent accuracy which couples will remain married and which will divorce within four to six years years. His best-selling book, *The Seven Principles for Making Marriage Work*, provides coupleship enhancing ideas. From his research, he sees that couples live too long in misery before seeking to make a change or seeking advice. He notes that couples often unnecessarily begin discussions in an adversarial manner and too often accept hurtful behavior from their partners. Successful partnerships include mutual support, compliments, expressions of appreciation and an ability to disagree without escalation. One sex difference that Gottman reports is that women are typically open to accepting influence from their male partners. However, the relationship really flourishes when both partners are willing to be persuaded by the other.

The bottom line is that all relationships require time, energy and care. There is plenty of evidence that our primary relationship, ideally a marriage, sustains us to a high degree and deserves high-priority focus.

## 5. Create Your Village

It's affirming to see some fathers pushing baby strollers and taking parental leave. My Dad never saw the inside of a poopy diaper. It's a new era when the character, stay-at-home-dad Adam, is a regular comic strip feature. While childcare is going in the gender-equality direction, mothers, on the whole, are still the main family caregivers. Mothers, fathers and families are not meant to raise their children on their own. Many cultures past and present surround families with care and guidance. In the Sudan and Kenya, the midwife becomes like a second mother. When I was born, my aunts and grandmothers took over many of my mother's chores and remained entwined in my life until I left the farm. When any of the children needed a kind ear, we rode our bikes to grandmother's house…and there were no big bad wolves along the way.

*Families with children need a community to lovingly encircle them.*

Now, we see grandmas behind the cash register at Tim Horton's or the bank manager's desk. The reality is that grandparents are often re-establishing new careers, taking university classes, traveling or living several provinces or states away. Still, families need a support circle that provides non-judgmental encouragement, helps nurture the children and empowers parents to feel powerful and competent. Hillary Clinton thoroughly describes this need in her book, *It Takes A Village*:

## Ten Tips for Single Moms

*"I might be a solo parent but I don't have to do it all alone."*

1. Remember that *Super Mom* is not even a comic book character!
2. Be open with your children. Tell them the truth or a childlike version of it. Children sense everything but they don't always know the questions to ask.
3. Remind children that you are human and have needs too. "You like going to the park, I like getting my nails done."
4. Insist that children contribute. When they say, "It's not fair!" let them know that life isn't always fair for you either. "It's not fair that I have to do everything when there are two other pairs of hands and legs in the house."
5. You are the shining example of how a successful woman behaves and what kind of response she accepts from others, including men.
6. Provide routines that children can count on.
7. During a job interview, find a way to mention your family. That way, there are no surprises. You also get a chance to learn more about your boss, the organization and their values. This provides you with more personal power! Choose a family-friendly organization.
8. Single moms have little downtime. Let your car or bus be your wind-down time. Sit in your car at a park or somewhere private between work and child-care pickup. Listen to music, have your coffee or be with your thoughts and decisions. Arrange for girlfriend phone chats after the children are in bed. Plan meals as a stress reliever. If cooking is a chore, have sporadic cereal nights.
9. Have a portrait taken of your *new family*. The depth that picture will have is priceless. Leane's picture of herself with her two girls sits on a shelf fixed between two angels. "It constantly serves as a reminder that I survived, had happy times and that difficult times can change for the better. That portrait still brings tears to my eyes. I am so proud of us all!"
10. Remember, it takes a village to raise a child—you can't do it all alone.

*Source*: LEANE RILEY

Children exist in the world as well as in the family. From the moment they are born, they depend on a host of other grown-ups—grandparents, neighbors, teacher, ministers, employers, political leaders, and untold others who touch their lives directly and indirectly… Each of us plays a part in every child's life. It takes a village to raise a child.

Everyday duties and demands can become exasperating with no one immediately available to share the load. Too often, single parents who are responsible for bringing in the only income feel inadequate and alone in their most important job of raising children. With so many demands, regrettably, they can easily become isolated from their previous circle of connections, even from their daily workmates and colleagues.

To ease the load, consider the following ideas:

- Take what parental leave is available to you.
- If you are nursing your baby, get support from La Leche League.
- If family is unavailable for regular support, *adopt* an *aunt, uncle* or *grandparent* from your neighborhood or place of worship.
- Have potluck meals or fun outings with other families.
- If you are solo parenting, consider applying for a Big Sister or Big Brother.
- Become a "team player" with your child's day care workers and teachers.
- Keep your career eye open for *child-friendly* organizations where the hours are flexible and/or childcare is onsite.
- Create a community that supports rather than stresses your family. If carpooling rides to the office or scheduling children's activities becomes too challenging, give yourself permission to make alternate plans. We must be kind to both ourselves and our children.

## 6. Give Up Your Grudge

Years ago, I was hired as a therapist at a private clinic by a very charismatic and attractive woman. Like a child at a chocolate factory, I felt excited and impressed with the extensive library of self-help books, articles, audio resources and group therapy rooms with light dimmers. Quickly, I was leading groups, providing couple and individual therapy with an extensive client base. However, within two weeks, like a slow car tire leak, my admiration and enthusiasm diminished. The woman routinely gossiped about clients to other clients. She decided clients who couldn't afford individual therapy were candidates for group work. She decided clients who had a lucrative income needed intense individual therapy. Horrors!

*Forgiving others is one of the greatest gifts you can give yourself.*

When I resigned, she decided that I had *betrayed her*. She believed she would lose many of her clients regardless of my resolve to fully withdraw from all involvement with this *healing* centre. And yes, I felt betrayed by finding myself in a moral and ethical dilemma of her creating. My dream job turned into a nightmare. Some people, regrettably, stay loyal when it would be far wiser for them to *wake up*, feel deceived and move on. As cultural observer and best-selling author, Gail Sheehy, said, "If an intelligent person is betrayed repeatedly and humiliated publicly, yet chooses to remain in that situation, one must ask: what are the rewards?" Sometimes, it is a paycheck. Other times, it is avoiding the anxiety of starting over again or avoiding confrontation itself.

When it comes to forgiveness, the most important person to forgive is yourself. We need to learn to forgive ourselves for our humanness, our misplaced trust, our leaning, our neediness and our innocence and naïveté. Certainly, forgiving both ourselves and the perpetrator of our harm frees us to totally move on.

The first place to start is with our feelings and ourselves. Identifying feelings and how they might be familiar allows us to be authentic with ourselves. We can learn to trust our intuition, not tolerate initial disrespects, heed first warning signals and trust ourselves to trust again. We can discern what action we need to take to reclaim our power. We might enlist a lawyer, write a letter (mail it or not), have a face-to-face confrontation or sell the company trophy at our next garage sale.

Too often, feelings of hurt and resentment disrupt our thoughts, invade our primary relationships, are taken into sleepless nights and sabotage our work performance. As therapist and women's resiliency expert, Beth Miller, wrote:

> As the adage says, resentment is like taking poison and then waiting for the other person to die. We who hold the memory (consciously or not) and the thoughts and feelings of the transgression, are the ones who are suffering, and we are the only ones who have the power to transcend the heaviness.

In order to come to a state of calm and peace, we have to stop pointing our finger in angry indignation. Healer, Gwendolyn Jansma, says, "You can trust other people to live life their way." In other words, note people's tendencies and the repeated behaviors that reveal their character. Stop depending on others to create your *happy ever after*.

## Ten Tips for Moving toward Forgiveness

*"I've let go of the hurt and learned to be discerning."*

1. Trust yourself, your observations and gut feelings.
2. Trust yourself to deal with challenging situations more than trusting others to change their habitual patterns to suit you.
3. Get honest with yourself and others. Hold others responsible for their part in the problem.
4. Speak up about what you consider acceptable and unacceptable behavior. Say, "This doesn't work for me."
5. Listen to and embrace your feelings of hurt and anger.
6. Notice the cost of feeling angry and resentful. Notice how much energy is drained by carrying the pain and the mental rerun of the betrayal. Notice what you are missing by hanging on.
7. Ask yourself, "What would life be like if I let go of this resentment?"
8. Where and when appropriate, turn your feelings of resentment and anger into constructive action. Confront the offender, make a formal complaint. In rare cases, go to court.
9. Make a choice to let go and lighten up rather than staying committed to misery.
10. Learn that forgiveness is a gift to yourself.

Trust your own observations of what people say and do. Accept this information as an accurate indicator about how they will behave in the future. Notice how often *Ellen* comes late to work and yet her co-workers act surprised week after week. Trust *Ellen's* behaviors, not her *excuses*.

Further to this discussion, Dr. Beth Hedva, author of *Betrayal, Trust and Forgiveness*, identified five common reactions to betrayal:

- A call for vengeance, vindication or retribution that leads to obsession about the betrayal
- Demonizing or dehumanizing the betrayer
- Generalizing the negative to others through stereotyping, prejudice and bigotry
- Self-betrayal—where we no longer trust ourselves or our judgment
- Suspicion, fear, control and manipulation to protect against future betrayals

Give up these initial reactions by moving towards forgiveness. You might even find yourself singing the line from *Can You Forgive Her*: "Or do you want revenge? But that's childish, so childish!"

## 7. Seek an Inclusive and Respectful Workplace

Like Roxy Anderson, we all perform better when we work for organizations where we are welcomed, supported and appreciated. Three survey respondents reported dealing with sexism. A woman with First Nations origin wrote that her biggest workplace challenge was "Being Aboriginal and viewed as different." It was my honor to work for a year in an ESL (English as a Second Language) program and another year as staff for an aboriginal family support centre. I was exposed to spiritual beliefs, foods, rituals and traditions that opened my eyes and heart to the many ways we have to express our humanness. I also learned that misunderstandings can more easily occur when people from diverse perspectives try to connect. Assumptions can become workplace poison. Yet, interest, openness and desire to connect can mend and bring cohesiveness.

Fearing differences makes about as much sense as this line from comedian, Rita Rudner. "I wonder if other dogs think poodles are members of a weird religious cult."

Great workplaces commit to inclusion programs to keep all employees accountable to act with respect and appreciation. These criteria are used by *Fortune* and *Working Mother* magazines when they annually choose their picks for best workplaces.

As individuals, there are small and significant behaviors we can exercise to create care and respectfulness. I looked to three sources to provide tips for inclusiveness and respect:

- a workshop with Tara Maniar, a diversity educator
- a workshop with Stephen Hammond, lawyer turned human rights expert and author of *Managing Human Rights at Work: 101 Practical Tips to Prevent Human Rights Disasters*
- conversations with my hubby, Les, a corporate ombuds

## Ten Tips for Inclusiveness and Respect

*"Welcome! You belong here."*

1. Embrace the changing demographics in North America. Our workforce and communities are increasingly more dependent on and benefit from immigrants from around the world.

2. Notice when your perceptions, beliefs, words and behaviors are offensive to others.

3. Be willing to apologize if you offend or wound another. Defending your position does the opposite of building an inclusive atmosphere. "You're too sensitive," sounds like, and is, *insensitive*.

4. Realize people cannot see, hear or guess your intentions. They only hear your words and see your actions.

5. Acknowledge that we often cluster in the company of like-minded people.

6. Many workplaces have a *tolerance* policy. Take the highroad and ask yourself, "Would I want others to *tolerate* me?" Do what you can to move you and your organization from *tolerance* to *respect*. Then consider moving to *appreciation* and finally to *celebration* of differences.

7. Celebrate both differences and similarities! This can include sharing traditional foods, celebrating a variety of religious and cultural holidays and taking an interest in another's rituals and customs.

8. Listen with curiosity to those who appear or sound different from you. Consider each person as a *cultural (background) entity unto themselves*.

9. If you are the recipient of discrimination or harassment, it is imperative that you don't give in. Do not believe the shaming, blaming and demeaning messages and comments. Note that they often come from those *addicted* to being in power-over positions. If asserting your rights doesn't get you the support you deserve, resign or access the Humans Rights Commission. But remember that simply having your feelings hurt might not warrant a human rights complaint.

10. Notice what you can do to create increased trust, belonging and appreciation at your organization's next meeting. Then act on your observations.

# Conclusion

My wish for you is to move from Woe to WOW, to know yourself as a WOW-Empowered woman and to find ways to live more vibrantly and resiliently. You may find yourself acting with everyday heroism at your workplace. As you do so you will model:

- Adversity can be an opportunity to exercise internal and relational resources.
- We can decide what we want to do and how we want to be.
- We don't have to stay stuck. We are not victims.
- Setbacks, mistakes and losses can transform into valuable learning experiences.
- We have more choices than we often realize or act upon.
- Resilience can be strengthened.
- Most of us are stronger than we think!

Not only that, one clear-skied day you will wake, look around and know how strong you really are. Jayne Relaford Brown described this beautifully in her poem *Finding Her Here:*

> I am becoming the woman I've wanted…
> cracked up by life
> with a laugh that's known bitter
> but, past it, got better,
> knows she's a survivor—
> that whatever comes,
> she can outlast it.

And so can you!

# Endnotes

**Introduction**

The Carrots, Eggs and Coffee Beans story is based on an email message forwarded to the author.

## I · About Resilience

Job Stress, The American Institute of Stress. (n.d.). Retrieved May 19, 2009, from <http://www.stress.org/job.htm>.

Morgan, P. with Morgan, K. (2000). *Love her as she is: Lessons from a daughter stolen by addictions*. Calgary, AB: Light Hearted Concepts. [Describes the author's story of struggling to connect in a challenging relationship and learning to love unconditionally with clear boundaries.]

Werner, E. & Smith R. (2001). *Journeys from childhood to midlife: Risk, resilience, and recovery*. Ithaca, NY: Cornell University Press.

Emmy Werner, Wikipedia. Retrieved May 19, 2009, from <http://en.wikipedia.org/wiki/Emmy_Werner>.

Joyce S. J. (2007). *Teaching an anthill to fetch: Developing collaborative intelligence @work*. Airdrie, AB: Mighty Small Books.

## II · Evaluate Your Resilience

**Internal Resilience:**

An electronic version of Score Your Resilience is available at <http://www.solutions forresilience.com>.

**External Support:**

**Resilience-Building Families and Homes**

Dove Campaign for Real Beauty. Retrieved May 19, 2009, from <http://www. campaignforrealbeauty.com>

**Resilience-Building Workplaces:**

Nan Henderson is President of Resiliency In Action and the creator of a resiliency model for children and youth used worldwide. Retrieved September 4, 2008, from <http://www.resiliency.com>.

Combs, A. (2008). *The living workplace: Soul, spirit and success in the 21st century*. Scarborough, ON: HarperCollins Publishers Canada. [The author attended an inspiring workshop by Ann Combs, May, 2008.]

100 best companies to work for. Retrieved May 19, 2009, from <**http://money.cnn.com/magazines/fortune/bestcompanies/2008**>.

100 best companies to work for in America, *Great* Place to Work® Institute, Inc. Retrieved May 19, 2009, from <**http://greatplacetowork.com/best/ list-bestusa-2008.htm**>.

[This site explains the criteria used by the Institute to produce the Fortune 100 Best Companies to Work For list and archives lists from previous years.]

## III · Demonstrations of Resilience at Work

### The Resilience-Generating Questions

Siebert, A. (2005). *The resiliency advantage: Master change, thrive under pressure, and bounce back from setbacks*. San Francisco, CA: Berrett-Koehler. [Dr Siebert, a researcher in surviving and resilience, was supportive and encouraging to the author. Sadly Dr. Siebert died in June 2009. He will be fondly remembered.]

Stern, E.S. (1992). *Running on empty: Meditations for indispensable women*. New York, NY: Bantam Dell Publishing Group.

### Name Your Woes

Maslow, A. (1987). *Motivation and personality*. New York, NY: HarperCollins. [Maslow died in 1970. He was one of the first psychologists to take an interest in human potential. His work was at the forefront of Humanistic Psychology and Positive Psychology.]

### WOW Empowered Stories – Internal Woes

### 1. Self-Doubt

Rosenberg, J., Rand, M. & Asay, D. (2000). *Body, self, & soul: Sustaining integration*, Atlanta, GA: Humanics Limited. [The author trained with these psychotherapists in Integrative Body Psychotherapy.]

### 2. Despair

Campbell, D. (2007). *If you don't know where you're going, you'll probably end up somewhere else*. Notre Dame, IN: Sorin Books.

### 3. Guilt

Gray, J. (2004). *Men are from Mars, women are from Venus*. New York, NY: HarperCollins.

**4. Workaholism**

Hochschild, A. (1989). *The second shift*. Clifton, Bristol, UK: Avon Books.

Philipson, I. (2002). *Married to the job: Why we live to work and what we can do about it*. New York, NY: Free Press, Simon & Schuster.

**5. Perfectionism**

Marano, E. H. (2008, May/April). The pitfalls of perfectionism. *Psychology Today*. Retrieved May 19, 2009, from <**http://www.psychologytoday.com/articles index.php?term= 20080225-000002&page=1**>.

**6. Physical Limitations**

Workplace injuries and illnesses in 2007, Economic News Release, Bureau of Labor Statistics, United States Department of Labor (2008, October 23). Retrieved May 19, 2009, from <**http://www.bls.gov/news.release/osh.nr0.htm**>.

**7. Learning Differences (Disability)**

Convention on the Rights of Persons with Disabilities. United Nations, Secretariat for the Convention on the Rights of Persons with Disabilities (2006). Retrieved May 19, 2009, from <**http://www.un.org/disabilities/convention/convention full.shtml**>.

**8. Focus on Weaknesses**

Buckingham, M. & Clifton, D. (2002). *Now, discover your strengths: How to develop your talents and those of the people you manage*. New York, NY: Free Press, Simon & Schuster.

Kapor Klein, F. (2007) Giving *notice: Why the best and brightest are leaving the workplace and how you can help them stay*. San Francisco, CA: Jossey-Bass.

**9. Lack of Education and Experience**

**10. Self-Silencing**

Parker-Pope, T. (2007, October 2). Marital spats, taken to heart. *New York Times*. Retrieved May 19, 2009, from <**http://www.nytimes.com/2007/10/02/health/ 02well.html?_r=1&scp=1&sq=Marital%20Spats,%20Taken%20to%20Heart&st =cse**>.

**WOW Empowered Stories – External Woes**

**1. Criticism**

Ryan, K.D. & Oeskreich, D.K. (1998). *Driving fear out of the workplace: Creating the high-trust, high-performance organization*. San Francisco, CA: Jossey-Bass.

**2. Blame**

**3. Verbal Abuse/Bullying**

Bell, A. (2005). *You can't talk to me that way! Stopping toxic language in the workplace*. Franklin Lakes, NJ: Career Press.

Cade, V. (2008). *Bully free at work*. Calgary AB: Performance Curve International Co. Valerie offers training on dealing with workplace bullying.

Stop Workplace Bullying! California Healthy Workplace Advocates (n.d.). Retrieved May 19, 2009, from <**http://www.bullyfreeworkplace.org**>.

Cade, V. (n.d.). How to have a bully free workplace. Retrieved May 19, 2009, from <**http://www.howtohaveabullyfreeworkplace.com**>.

U.S. workplace bullying survey, September 2007, Workplace Bullying Institute & Zogby International. Retrieved May 19, 2009, from <**http://bullyinginstitute.org/research.html**>.

Futterman, S. (2004). *When you work for a bully: Assessing your options and taking action*. Leonia, NJ: Croce Publishing Group.

Stringer, H. (2001, February 12). Raging Bullies. *Nurse Week*. Retrieved May 19, 2009, from <**http://www.nurseweek.com/news/features/01-02/bully.asp**>.

**4. Sexual Harassment/Assault**

Gordon Howard, L. (2007). *The sexual harassment handbook*. Franklin Lakes, NJ: Career Press.

**5. Sexism**

Fuller, G. (1996). *The workplace survival guide: Tips and techniques for succeeding on the job*. Upper Saddle River, NJ: Prentice Hall.

Rubin, H. (2008, March 17). Sexism. *Condé Nast Portfolio*. Retrieved May 19, 2009, from <**http://www.portfolio.com/executives/features/2008/03/17/Sexism-in-the-Workplace**>.

Farrell, W. (2005). *Why men earn more: The startling truth behind the pay gap—And what women can do about it*. New York, NY: American Management Association.

**6. Intolerance**

Herring, H.B. (2005, July 24). There's no shortage of intolerance in the workplace. *New York Times*. Retrieved May 19, 2009, from <**http://www.nytimes.com/2005/07/24/business/yourmoney/24count.html**>.

**7. Moral Dilemma**

Popov, L. (2000). *The virtues project*. Fawnskin, CA: Jalmar Press. [Learn about 52 virtues or what Popov calls, "The Gifts of Character." The author has taken Virtues Project training, a program that brings out the best character in people of all ages.]

## 8. Business Betrayal

## 9. Spousal Betrayal

*Divorce Rate.* (n.d.). Retrieved May 19, 2009, from <**http://www.divorcerate.org**>. This site has statistics on divorce from the United States, Canada and other countries.

## 10. Caregiver Demands

Bibby, R.W. (2005, February 10). Child Care Aspirations (Press Release), The Vanier Institute of the Family. Retrieved May 19, 2009, from <**http://www.vifamily.ca/ newsroom/press_feb_10_05_c.html**>.

Public Agenda (2000, August 22). Parents of young children yearn to be home to care for them, show wide-ranging distrust of day care centers (Press Release). Retrieved May 19, 2009, from <**http://www.publicagenda.org/press-releases/ parents-young-children-yearn-be-home-care-them-show-wide-ranging- distrust-day-care-centers**>.

## Solo Mom Isolation

Fleury, D. (2008, May). Low-income children. *Perspectives* (Statistics Canada). Retrieved May 19, 2009, from <**http://www.statcan.gc.ca/pub/75-001-x/ 2008105/pdf/10578-eng.pdf**>.

Shepell•fgi. (2006, May 8). Employers need to focus on 'top seven' drivers of employee engagement and retention to improve organizational success (Press Release). Retrieved May 19, 2009, from <**http://www.shepellfgi.com/EN-US/ AboutUs/News/News%20 and%20Media%20Releases/media20060508. asp**>.

# IV · Strengthening Your Resilience

## I · Protect Your Inner WOW Woman

## 1. Establish Clear Boundaries

Katherine, A. (1993). *Boundaries: Where you end and I begin.* New York, NY: Free Press, Simon & Schuster.

The author's training in Integrative Body Psychotherapy and Hakomi instilled the importance of clear boundaries.

## 2. Align with Integrity

Lacayo, R. & Ripley, A. (2002, December 22). Cynthia Cooper, Coleen Rowley and Sherron Watkins—Persons of the Year 2002. *Time*. Retrieved May 19, 2009, from **<http://www.time.com/time/subscriber/personoftheyear/2002/poyintro.html>**.

Kennedy-Glans, D. & Schulz, R. (2005). *Corporate integrity: A toolkit for managing beyond compliance*. Hoboken, NJ: Wiley. [Donna Kennedy-Glans models working internationally with integrity.]

Thomson, Calum (updated 2009, April 24). *RIP Taylor—Four-Way Test*. Retrieved May 19, 2009, from **<http://www.rotaryfirst100.org/presidents/1954taylor/taylor/essay.htm>**.

## 3. Keep Your *Humanness*

Steinem, G. (1995). *Moving beyond words: Age, rage, sex, power, money, muscles: Breaking the boundaries of gender*. New York, NY: Free Press, Simon & Schuster. [The author has been to two lectures by Steinem and both times walked away feeling proud to be a woman.]

Morgan, P. with Morgan, K. (2004). *Love her as she is: Lessons from a daughter stolen by addictions*. Calgary AB: Light Hearted Concepts. [The author's journey with a vulnerable daughter.]

## 4. Embrace Your *Womanness*

Tannen, D. (1991). *You just don't understand me: Women and men in conversation*. New York, NY: Ballantine Books.

Grymes, S. & Stantan, M. (1993). *Coping with the male ego in the workplace*. Stamford, CT: Longmeadow Press.

## 5. First, Care for the Mother

Salary.com. (2006, May 2). What is a mom worth? Working mom vs. stay at home mom salaries for 2006 (Press Release). Retrieved May 19, 2009, from **<http://www.salary.com/aboutus/layoutscriptsabtl_default.asp?tab=abt&cat= cat 012&ser=ser041&part=Par481&isdefault=0>**.

Power, W. (2003, April 16). More women stressed out by work, families says Dalhousie University study. The University of Toronto, Childcare Resource and Research Unit website focuses on Canadian child care research and policy. Retrieved May 19, 2009, from **<http://action.web.ca/home/crru/rsrcs_crru_full.shtml?x=33519&AA_ EX_Session=40e207919755a884e4cc255c16a4264b>**.

The Canadian Institute of Stress offers a tele-class called, "Pampering the Woman Within...finding balance in a stressful world" at <**http://www.stresscanada. org/pamper.html**>. [It is also a good source of statistics on distress. Retrieved October 5, 2008, from <**http://www.stresscanada.org**>.]

**6. Choose *Your* Best Life Rhythm**

To subscribe to Beverley Smith's "WHO CARES? Recent Research on Caregiving" e-newsletter, write to <**bevgsmith@alumni.ucalgary.ca**>.

**7. Get Familiar with Protective Laws**

Bill H-6: Canadian Human Rights Act, Department of Justice, Canada (current to 2009, March 29). Retrieved May 19, 2009, from <**http://laws.justice.gc.ca/en/ ShowFullDoc/cs/H-6///en**>.

## II · Nurture Your WOWness

**1. Put Pollyanna to Shame: Think Optimistically**

McGraw, Dr. P. (2008, September). Free yourself from fear. *Ladies Home Journal.* Retrieved May 19, 2009, from <**http://www.lhj.com/health/stress/relaxation- techniques/free-yourself-from-fear/**>.

Seligman, M. (1998). *Learned optimism: How to change your mind and your life.* New York, NY: Free Press, Simon & Schuster.

**2. Sweet-Talk to Yourself**

Carson, R. (2003). *Taming your gremlin: A surprisingly simple method for getting out of your own way.* San Francisco, CA: HarperSanFrancisco.

**3. Honor Your Feelings**

Pollock, W. (1999). *Real boys: Rescuing our sons from the myths of boyhood.* New York, NY: Owl Books, Macmillan.

**4. Move Out of Painful Feelings**

Goleman, D. (1997). *Emotional intelligence: Why it can matter more than IQ.* New York, NY: Bantam Dell Publishing Group.

**5. Have a *Good* Cry**

Frey, W. (1985). *Crying: The mystery of tears.* Minneapolis, MN: Winston Press.

Kubler-Ross, E. (1997). *On death and dying.* New York, NY: Scribner, Simon & Shuster.

**6. Lighten Up!**

Lefcourt, H. (2000). *Humor: The psychology of living buoyantly* (The Plenum Series in Social/Clinical Psychology). New York, NY: Springer.

Barreca, R. (1991). *They used to call me Snow White but I drifted: Women's strategic use of humor.* Adams, MA: Viking.

Mackoff, B. (1990). *What Mona Lisa knew: A woman's guide to getting ahead in business by lightening up.* Lowell, MA: Lowell House.

Kerr, M. (2006). *Inspiring workplaces: Creating the kind of workplace where everyone wants to work.* Humour at Work Institute. [The author refers to a 2003 issue of Harvard Business Review about executives using humor. This is one of best books for ideas for increasing humor in the workplace.]

### 7. Attend to Your Body

Roizen, M., Oz, M., Oz, L. & Spiker, T. (2005). *You: The owner's manual: An insider's guide to the body that will make you healthier and younger.* London, UK: HarperCollins.

See the reference in these endnotes under "First Care for *the Mother*" for the tele-class offered by The Canadian Institute of Stress.

## III · Communicate with WOW Power

### 1. Be a Dear with Two Ears: Listen

Covey, S. (1990). *7 habits of highly effective people.* New York: NY: Free Press, Simon & Schuster.

Trinity College (n.d.) Listening. Retrieved January 13, 2009, from <**http://www.trinity.wa.edu.au/plduffyrc/library/study/listen.htm**>. [Note: This link is no longer active.]

### 2. Speak Up: Assert or You'll Blurt

Bloom, L., Coburn, K. & Pearlman, J.C. (2000). *The new assertive woman.* Center City, MN: Wellness Institute, Hazelden.

Phelps, S. & Austin, N. (2002). *The assertive woman.* Cottesloe, WA: Impact.

### 3. Breathe and Get Grounded

Richo, D. (2002). *How to be an adult in relationships: The five keys to mindful loving.* Boston, MA: Shambhala.

Eddy, W. (2007). *High conflict people in legal disputes.* Scottsdale, AZ: High Conflict Institute.

### 4. Ease Conflict

Coloroso, B. (2007). *Extraordinary evil: Why genocide happens.* New York, NY: Nation Books.

Coloroso, B. (2005). *The bully, the bullied and the bystander: From preschool to secondary schoolæHow parents and teachers can help break the cycle of violence.* London, UK. Piccadilly Press Ltd.

### 5. Plan for Resolution

Fisher, R., Ury, W. & Patton, B. (1992). *Getting to yes: Negotiating agreement without giving in.* Boston, MA: Houghton Mifflin. [This is the classic book on conflict negotiation.]

Rosenberg, M. (2003). *Nonviolent communication: A language of life.* Encinitas, CA: Puddle Dancer Press.

### 6. Filter Criticism: Offer Feedback

Simon, S. (1979). *Negative criticism and what you can do about it…* Allen, TX: Argus Communications.

Charvet, S.R. (n.d.). *The feedback sandwich is out to lunch.* Retrieved May 19, 2009, from <**http://www.successstrategies.com/news-and-media/articles-interviews/Feedback _sandwich.php**>.

### 7. Manage Management

Ng, T.W.H., Sorensen, K.L. & Eby, L.T. (2006, September 22: Volume 27, Issue 8). Locus of control at work: A meta-analysis. *Journal of Organizational Behavior.* Retrieved May 19, 2009, from <**http://www3.interscience.wiley.com/journal/113344428/abstract**>.

Low percentage of Canadians 'fully engaged' at work. (2005, November 15). *Ottawa Business Journal.* Retrieved May 19, 2009, from <**http://www.ottawabusinessjournal.com/284714241260955.php**>. [This article refers to a study conducted by Towers Perrin HR Services.]

Willis, G. (2005, March 29). How to Manage Your Manager. *CNNMoney.com.* Retrieved May 19, 2009, from <**http://money.cnn.com/2005/03/16/pf/saving/willis_tips/index.htm**>.

Markham, U. (1998). *How to deal with difficult people.* New York, NY: Thorsons, HarperCollins.

IV · Take WOW Action: You Can Do It!

### 1. Champion Change

Brooks, R. and Goldstein, S. (2004). *The power of resilience: Achieving balance, confidence, and personal strength in your life.* Columbus, OH: McGraw-Hill.

Everett Rogers, Wikipedia. Retrieved May 19, 2009, from <**http://en.wikipedia.org/ wiki/Everett_Rogers**>.

Kotter, J. (2002). *The heart of change: Real-life stories of how people change their organizations.* Boston, MA: Harvard Business School Press.

## 2. Acknowledge and Demonstrate Your Strengths

Peterson, C. & Seligman, M. (2004). *Character strengths and virtues: A handbook and classification.* Oxford, UK: Oxford University Press.

Take the Myers-Briggs Type Indicator® inventory of your personality preferences (extroverted or introverted, sensing or intuitive, feeling or thinking and judging or perceiving). Retrieved April 25, 2009, from <**http://www.myersbriggs.org/ my-mbti-personality-type/**>.

Buckingham, M. & Clifton, D. (2002). *Now, discover your strengths: How to develop your talents and those of the people you manage.* New York, NY: Free Press, Simon & Schuster.

Take Dr. Martin Seligman's VIA Signature Strengths Questionnaire. Retrieved April 25, 2009, from <**http://www.authentichappiness.sas.upenn.edu/Default. aspx**>.

## 3. *Make Up Your Mind,* Decide

Maltz, M. (2002). *New Psycho-Cybernetics.* Saddle River, NJ: Prentice Hall Press. [The phrase, "21-Day Habit" and the original Psycho-Cybernetics book were published in 1960.]

Scott, S. (2002). *Fierce conversations: Achieving success at work and in life, one conversation at a time.* New York, NY: Penguin Group.

## 4. Demonstrate Courage

Huffington, A. (2006). *On becoming fearless... in love, work, and life.* New York, NY: Little, Brown and Company.

Jana Stanfield composes and sings inspirational and uplifting songs. Song titles include *What Would I do Today If I Were Brave, I'm Not Lost, I'm Exploring* and *Everyday Greatness Every Day.* Retrieved April 25, 2009, from <**http://www. janastanfield.com**>.

## 5. Go Back to School, *Maybe*

Comaford-Lynch, C. (2007). *Rules for renegades: How to make more money, rock your career, and revel in your individuality.* Columbus, OH: McGraw-Hill. [This high-school drop-out has built and sold five of her own businesses, has invested in over 200 startup companies, including Google, and consulted to the White House (Clinton and Bush), 700 of the Fortune 1000, and over 3000 small businesses.]

Sher, B. (1995). *I could do anything if I only knew what it was: How to discover what you really want and how to get it.* New York, NY: Dell Publishing. [Sher also wrote *Wishcraft: How to Get What You Really Want* (Ballantine Books, 1984) and started *Success Teams* with members helping each other reach their goals. Visit Sher on her website. Retrieved April 25, 2009, from <**http://www.shersuccess teams.com**>.]

**6. Be Laid Off without Laying Down**

**7. Quit or Resign**

Kapor Klein, F. (2007). *Giving notice: Why the best and the brightest are leaving the workplace and how you can help them stay.* San Francisco, CA: Jossey-Bass.

Quinlan, M.L. (2005). *Time off for good behavior: How hardworking women can take a break and change their lives.* New York, NY: Broadway Books.

Kanchier, C. (2008). *Dare to change your job and your life.* Calgary, AB: Questers. [An exploration of the advantages of being "questers," people who take charge of their goals and life.]

## V · Connect for Added WOW Power

**1. Give and Receive Acknowledgement**

Rath, T. & Clifton, D. (2007). *How full is your bucket? Positive strategies for work and life.* Washington, DC: Gallup Press. [Rath's idea of filling your and others' buckets is similar to the idea of an emotional piggy bank.]

Kouzes, J.M. & Posner, B.Z. (2003). *Encouraging the heart: A leader's guide to rewarding and recognizing others.* San Francisco, CA: Jossey-Bass.

Kaye, B. & Jordan-Evans, S. (2008). *Love 'em or lose 'em: Getting good people to stay.* San Francisco, CA: Berrett-Koehler.

Appreciative Inquiry, Wikipedia. Retrieved May 19, 2009, from <**http://en.wikipedia.org/wiki/Appreciative_Inquiry**>. [Appreciative Inquiry is a particular way of asking questions that fosters positive relationships and builds on the pluses and strengths in a person, a situation or an organization.]

Hammond, S.A. (1998). *The thin book of appreciative inquiry.* Bend, OR: Thin Book.

B.F. Skinner was the pioneer in Behavioral Therapy. Retrieved November 23, 2008, from <**http://www.bfskinner.org**>.

### 2. Be a Brazen Gal: Self Promote

McAleavy, T. (2004, August 22). Men far outshine women at self-promotion. *Miami Herald*. Retrieved January 13, 2009, from <**http://www.isrsurveys.com/en/pdf/ media/Miami%20Herald-Men%20far%20outshine%20women%20at%20 self-promotion.pdf**>. [Note: This link is no longer active.]

### 3. Get a Little Help from Your Friends

Taylor, E.S. (2002). *The tending instinct: How nurturing is essential to who we are and how we live*. New York, NY: Times Books, Macmillan.

Rath, T. (2006). *Vital friends: The people you can't afford to live without*. Washington, DC: Gallup Press.

### 4. Nurture a Supportive Love Relationship

Adams, M. (2005, April 2). Married couples share happiness more than cohabitating couples. *NaturalNews.com*. This article refers to research by Nick Powdthavee. Retrieved May 19, 2009, from <**http://www.naturalnews.com/006267.html**>.

Waite, L. & Gallagher, M. (2001). *The case for marriage: Why married people are happier, healthier, and better off financially*. New York, NY: Broadway Books.

Gottman, J. & Silver, N. (2000). *Seven principles for making marriage work: A practical guide from the country's foremost relationship expert*. New York, NY: Three Rivers Press.

Hitti, M. (2005, March 22). Recipe for Happiness in Marriage. *WebMD*. Retrieved May 19, 2009, from <**http://www.webmd.com/sex-relationships/news/20050322/ recipe-for-happiness-in-marriage**>.

### 5. Create Your Village

Rodham Clinton, H. (1996). *It takes a village*. New York, NY: Simon & Schuster.

La Leche League supports mothering through breastfeeding. Retrieved November 23, 2008, from <**http://www.llli.org**>.

Working Mother magazine is an excellent resource of support for employed mothers. Retrieved November 23, 2008, from <**http://www.workingmother.com**>.

Ellison, S. (2001). *The courage to be a single mother: Becoming whole again after divorce*. New York, NY: HarperCollins. [This book has been a mainstay for Leane Riley through her years of solo parenting.]

### 6. Give Up Your Grudge

The American writer and lecturer, Gail Sheehy is renowned for her writing on the life cycle. Retrieved November 29, 2008, from <**http://www.gailsheehy.com**>.

Miller, E. (2005). *The women's book of resilience*. Newburyport, MA: Conari Press.

Gwendolyn Jansma is more than a healer. She's a skilled therapist, intuitive and poet. Her books of poetry include *Sticks and Stones and Strawberries*. She mentored the author and leads Heart Seek Gatherings.

**7. Seek an Inclusive and Respectful Workplace**

Tara Maniar of Toronto, Ontario led a *diversity* workshop in Calgary, Alberta, which the author attended.

Hammond, S. (2004). *Managing human rights at work: 101 practical tips to prevent human rights disasters*. Vancouver, BC: Harassment Solutions Inc.

## Conclusion

Relaford Brown, J. (2004). *My first real tree* (A collection of poetry including, *Finding Her Here*). Kanona, NY: FootHills.

# Resources

Axelrod, A. & Holtje, J. (1997). *201 ways to say no gracefully and effectively*. Columbus, OH: McGraw-Hill.

Barreca, R. (1991). *They used to call me Snow White but I drifted: Women's strategic use of humor*. Adams, MA: Viking.

Beattie, M. (1990). *The language of letting go*. Center City, MN: Hazelden.

Bell, A. (2005). *You can't talk to me that way! Stopping toxic language in the workplace*. Franklin Lakes, NJ: Career Press.

Bloom, L., Coburn, K. & Pearlman, J.C. (2000). *The new assertive woman*. Center City, MN: Wellness Institute, Hazelden.

Brooks, R. & Goldstein, S. (2004). *The power of resilience: Achieving balance, confidence, and personal strength in your life*. Columbus, OH: McGraw-Hill.

Buckingham, M. (2007). *Go put your strengths to work: 6 powerful steps to achieve outstanding performance*. New York, NY: Free Press, Simon & Schuster.

———. (2005). *The one thing you need to know: . . . About great managing, great leading, and sustained individual success*. New York, NY: Free Press, Simon & Schuster.

Buckingham, M. & Coffman, C. (1999). *First, break all the rules: What the world's greatest managers do differently*. New York, NY: Simon & Schuster.

Buckingham, M. & Clifton, D. (2002). *Now, discover your strengths: How to develop your talents and those of the people you manage*. New York, NY: Free Press, Simon & Schuster.

Cade, V. (2008). *Bully free at work*. Calgary, AB: Performance Curve International Co.

Cameron, J., Bryan, M. & Allen, C. (1998). *The artist's way at work: Riding the dragon: Twelve weeks to creative freedom*. New York, NY: HarperCollins.

Campbell, D. (2007). *If you don't know where you're going, you'll probably end up somewhere else*. Notre Dame, IN: Sorin Books.

Canfield, J., Hansen, M.V. & Hewitt, L. (2000). *The power of focus*. Deerfield Beach, FL: Health Communication Inc (HCI).

Carson, R. (2003). *Taming your gremlin: A surprisingly simple method for getting out of your own way*. SanFrancisco, CA: HarperSanFrancisco.

Charvet, S.R. (1997). *Words that change minds: mastering the language of influence*. Dubuque, IA: Kendall/Hunt Publishing Company.

Clemmer, J. (2001). *The leader's digest: Timeless principles for team and organization success*. Kitchener , ON: The Clemmer Group.

Coloroso, B. (2007). *Extraordinary evil: Why genocide happens*. New York, NY: Nation Books.

———. (2005). *The bully, the bullied and the bystander: From preschool to secondary schoolæHow parents and teachers can help break the cycle of violence*. London, UK: Piccadilly Press Ltd.

Comaford-Lynch, C. (2007). *Rules for renegades: How to make more money, rock your career, and revel in your individuality*. Columbus, OH: McGraw-Hill.

Combs, A. (2001). *The living workplace: Soul, spirit and success in the 21st century*. Scarborough, ON: HarperCollins Publishers Canada.

Cornelius, H. (1998). *The gentle revolution: Men and women at work—what goes wrong and how to fix it*. Pymble, Australia: Simon & Schuster Australia.

Coutu, D. (2003). *How resilience works, Harvard Business Review on building personal and organizational resilience*. Boston, MA: Harvard Business School Press.

Covey, S. (1990). *7 habits of highly effective people*. New York, NY: Free Press, Simon & Schuster.

DeMars, N. (1998). *You want me to do what? When, where, and how to draw the line at work*. New York, NY: Simon & Schuster

Eddy, W. (2007). *High conflict people in legal disputes*. Scottsdale, AZ: High Conflict Institute.

Ellison, S. (2001). *The courage to be a single mother: Becoming whole again after divorce.* New York, NY: HarperCollins.

Enright, R.D. (2008). *Forgiveness is a choice: A step-by-step process for resolving anger and restoring hope*. Arlington, VA: American Psychological Association.

Farrell, W. (2005). *Why men earn more: The startling truth behind the pay gapæAnd what women can do about it*. New York, NY: American Management Association.

Fisher, R., Ury, W. & Patton, B. (1992). *Getting to yes: Negotiating agreement without giving in*. Boston, MA: Houghton Mifflin.

Fuller, G. (1996). *The workplace survival guide: Tips and techniques for succeeding on the job*. Upper Saddle River, NJ: Prentice Hall.

Foord Kirk, J. (2002). *Survivability: Career strategies for the new world of work*. Kelowna, BC: Kirkfoord Communications.

Futterman, S. (2004). *When you work for a bully: Assessing your options and taking action*. Leonia, NJ: Croce Publishing Group.

Frey, W. (1985). *Crying: The mystery of tears*. Minneapolis, MN: Winston Press.

Gottlieb, L. & Hyatt, C. (1993). *When smart people fail: Rebuilding yourself for success*. New York, NY: Penguin Group.

Goleman, D. (2006). *Social intelligence: The new science of human relationships*. New York, NY: Bantam Dell Publishing Group.

———. (1997). *Emotional intelligence: Why it can matter more than IQ*. New York, NY: Bantam Dell Publishing Group.

Gordon Howard, L. (2007). *The sexual harassment handbook*. Franklin Lakes, NJ: Career Press.

Gottman, J. & Silver, N. (2000). *Seven principles for making marriage work: A practical guide from the country's foremost relationship expert*. New York, NY: Three Rivers Press.

Gray, J. (2004). *Men are from Mars, women are from Venus*. New York, NY: HarperCollins.

Grymes, S. & Stantan, M. (1993). *Coping with the male ego in the workplace*. Stamford, CT: Longmeadow Press.

Hammond, S. (2004). *Managing human rights at work: 101 practical tips to prevent human rights disasters*. Vancouver, BC: Harassment Solutions Inc.

Hammond, S. A. (1998). *The thin book of appreciative inquiry*. Bend, OR: Thin Book.

Hedva, E. (2001). *Betrayal, trust, and forgiveness: A guide to emotional healing and self-renewal*. Berkeley, CA: Celestial Arts.

Helgesen, S. (1995). *The female advantage: Women's ways of leadership*. New York, NY: Broadway.

Hewitt, F. & Hewitt, L. (2003). *The power of focus for women*. Deerfield Beach, FL: Health Communication Inc (HCI).

Hochschild, A. (1989). *The second shift*. Bristol, UK: Avon Books.

Horn, S. (1997). *Tongue Fu! How to deflect, disarm, and defuse any verbal conflict*. New York: NY: St. Martin's Griffin.

Huffington, A. (2006). *On becoming fearless...in love, work, and life*. New York, NY: Little, Brown and Company.

Joyce, S.J. (2007). *Teaching an anthill to fetch: Developing collaborative intelligence @work*. Airdrie, AB: Mighty Small Books.

Kanchier, C. (2008). *Dare to change your job and your life*. Calgary, AB: Questers.

Kapor Klein, F. (2007). *Giving notice: Why the best and the brightest are leaving the workplace and how you can help them stay*. San Francisco, CA: Jossey-Bass.

Katherine, A. (1993). *Boundaries: Where you end and I begin*. New York, NY: Simon & Schuster.

Kaye, B. & Jordan-Evans, S. (2008). *Love 'em or lose 'em: Getting good people to stay (4th ed.)*. San Francisco, CA: Berrett-Koehler.

Kennedy-Glans, D. & Schulz, R. (2005). *Corporate integrity: A toolkit for managing beyond compliance*. Hoboken, NJ: Wiley.

Kerr, M. (2006). *Inspiring workplaces: Creating the kind of workplace where everyone wants to work*. Canmore, AB: Humour at Work Institute.

———. (2001). *You can't be serious! Putting humor to work*. Canmore, AB: Humor at Work Institute.

Kersey, C. (2005). *Unstoppable women: Achieve breakthrough goals in 30 days*. St. Emmaus, PA: Rodale.

Klaus, P. (2007). *The hard truth about soft skills: Workplace lessons smart people wish they'd learned sooner*. New York, NY: HarperCollins.

Kotter, J. (2002). *The heart of change: Real-life stories of how people change their organizations*. Boston, MA: Harvard Business School Press.

Kouzes, J.M., & Posner, B.Z. (2003). *Encouraging the heart: A leader's guide to rewarding and recognizing others*. San Francisco, CA: Jossey-Bass.

Kubler-Ross, E. (1997). *On death and dying*. New York, NY: Scribner, Simon & Shuster.

Lefcourt, H. (2000). *Humor: The Psychology of Living Buoyantly* (The Plenum Series in Social/Clinical Psychology). New York, NY: Springer.

Mackoff, B. (1991). *What Mona Lisa knew: A woman's guide to getting ahead in business by lightening up*. Lowell, MA: Lowell House.

Maltz, M. (2002). *New Psycho-Cybernetics*. Upper Saddle River, NJ: Prentice Hall.

Markham, U. (1998). *How to deal with difficult people*. New York, NY: Thorsons, HarperCollins.

Maslow, A. (1987). *Motivation and personality*. New York, NY: HarperCollins.

Miller, E. (2005). *The women's book of resilience*. Newburyport, MA: Conari Press.

Miller, P. (2004). *A little book of forgiveness: Challenges and meditations for anyone with something to forgive*. Berkeley CA: Fearless Books.

Mooney, N. (2005). *I can't believe she did that! Why women betray other women at work*. New York, NY: St. Martin Press.

Morgan, P. with Morgan, K. (2000). *Love her as she is: Lessons from a daughter stolen by addictions*. Calgary, AB: Light Hearted Concepts.

Morgenstern, J. (2004). *Making work work: New strategies for surviving and thriving at the office*. New York, NY: Simon & Schuster.

Myss, C. (2005). *Invisible acts of power*. New York, NY: Free Press, Simon & Schuster.

O'Gorman, P. (1994). *Dancing backwards in high heels: How women master the art of resilience.* Center City, MN: Hazelden.

Piven, J. (2003). *The worst-case scenario survival handbook: work.* San Francisco, CA: Chronicle Books.

Phelps, S. & Austin, N. (2002). *The assertive woman.* Cottesloe WA: Impact.

Philipson, I. (2002). *Married to the job: Why we live to work and what we can do about it.* New York, NY: Free Press, Simon & Schuster.

Pollock, W. (1999). *Real boys: Rescuing our sons from the myths of boyhood.* New York, NY: Owl Books, Macmillan.

Popov, L. (2000). *The virtues project.* Fawnskin, CA: Jalmar Press.

Quinlan, M.L. (2005). *Time off for good behavior: How hardworking women can take a break and change their lives.* New York, NY: Broadway Books.

Rath, T. (2006). *Vital friends: The people you can't afford to live without.* Washington, DC: Gallup Press.

Rath, T. & Clifton, D. (2007). *How full is your bucket? Positive strategies for work and life.* Washington, DC: Gallup Press.

Reivich, K. & Reivich, S. (2002). *The resilience factor: 7 essential skills for overcoming life's inevitable obstacles.* New York, NY: Broadway Books.

Richo, D. (2002). *How to be an adult in relationships: The five keys to mindful loving.* Boston, MA: Shambhala.

Rodham Clinton, H. (1996). *It takes a village.* New York, NY: Simon & Schuster.

Roizen, M., Oz, M., Oz, L., & Spiker, T. (2005). *You: The owner's manual: An insider's guide to the body that will make you healthier and younger.* New York, NY: HarperCollins.

Rosenberg, J., Rand, M. & Asay, D. (2000). *Body, self, & soul: Sustaining integration.* Atlanta, GA: Humanics Ltd.

Rosenberg, M. (2003). *Nonviolent communication: A language of life.* Encinitas, CA: Puddle Dancer Press.

Ryan, K.D. & Oeskreich, D.K. (1998). *Driving fear out of the workplace: Creating the high-trust, high-performance organization.* San Francisco, CA: Jossey-Bass.

Scott, S. (2002). *Fierce conversations: Achieving success at work and in life, one conversation at a time.* New York, NY: Penguin Group.

Seligman, M. (2004). *Authentic happiness: Using the new positive psychology to realize your potential for lasting fulfillment.* New York, NY: Free Press, Simon & Schuster.

———. (1998). *Learned optimism: How to change your mind and your life.* New York, NY: Free Press, Simon & Schuster.

Sher, B. (1995). *I could do anything if I only knew what it was: How to discover what you really want and how to get it.* New York, NY: Dell Publishing.

Siebert, A. (2005). *The resiliency advantage: Master change, thrive under pressure, and bounce back from setbacks.* San Francisco, CA: Berrett-Koehler.

———. (1996). *The survivor personality.* New York, NY: Perigee Books.

Simon, S. (1979). *Negative criticism and what you can do about it.* Allen, TX: Argus Communications.

Smedes, L.B. (2007). *Forgive and forget: Healing the hurts we don't deserve.* New York, NY: HarperCollins.

Stanwick, A. (2007). *Forgiveness, the mystery and miracle.* Calgary, AB: Heart Message.

Steinem, G. (1995). *Moving beyond words: Age, rage, sex, power, money, muscles: Breaking the boundaries of gender.* New York, NY: Simon & Schuster.

Stern, E.S. (1992). *Running on empty.* New York, NY: Bantam Dell Publishing Group.

Tannen, D. (1991). *You just don't understand me: Women and men in conversation.* New York, NY: Ballantine Books.

Taylor, E.S. (2002). *The tending instinct: How nurturing is essential to who we are and how we live.* New York, NY: Times Books, Macmillan.

Waite, L. & Gallagher, M. (2001). *The case for marriage: Why married people are happier, healthier, and better off financially.* New York, NY: Broadway.

Warner, E. & Smith, R. (2001). *Journeys from childhood to midlife: Risk, resilience, and recovery.* Ithaca, NY: Cornell University Press.

## Other Books by Patricia Morgan

*Love Her As She Is: Lessons from a Daughter Stolen by Addictions*
PATRICIA MORGAN MA, with KELLY MORGAN
A true story with 14 ways to demonstrate unconditional love.

"Patricia Morgan and her daughter have written a book that is searingly honest. …most important of all, there are solutions in this book—tools and techniques to move us all forward. This mother and daughter have been through hell. What they have to say can put out some of those hell-fires for you."
DR. SIDNEY B. SIMON, Professor Emeritus, University of Massachusetts
and author of *Values Clarification* among other books

～

*She Said: A Tapestry of Women's Quotes*
This collection of inspiring, wise and witty words of women
from the world makes a thoughtful gift.

"This is a fabulous tribute to women!"
FRANCES WRIGHT, Founder, *Famous 5 Foundation*

～

*Gag Your Nagging: 101+ Ways to Communicate More Effectively*
*& Enhance Family Cooperation & Harmony*

(available as an e-book at **www.solutionsforresilience.com**)

More than just a collection of the most common, infuriating and
downright funny nags that many of us are sometimes guilty of uttering,
*Gag Your Nagging* provides some strategies to get beyond the
crazy-making talk to more healthy and harmonious communication.

"A light-hearted yet profoundly helpful resource that helps you cool your jets,
get along better with others and have more fun."

SHARON HORSTEAD, certified Heal Your Life® workshop leader and coach

## Mini Books

*Frantic Free: 167 Ways to Calm Down and Lighten Up*
For those who find themselves too often feeling frantic, frenzied or simply fried.

"Most of us don't take the time for ourselves because we believe we're too busy or stressed! The tips from this fabulous booklet can help you 'de-stress for success' and find time for the things that matter."

MICHELLE CEDERBERG, MKin, PFLC,
*Live Out Loud Fitness & Wellness Consulting*

~

*The Light Hearted Approach: 87 Ways to Be an Upbeat Parent*
Parents can easily add fun and loving connection to their home life.

"It brilliantly combines valuable parenting tips with lots of ideas for family fun. It's a great resource."

KATHY LYNN, author of *How Parent Can Teach Children to Do the Right Thing*
and *Who's in Charge Anyway?*

~

*Alberta Women Said: Wise Words by Wondrous Western Women*
A perfect gift to honor a woman of Alberta.

"As we are what we eat, so we are what we speak! This collection helps all of us to enjoy being women and renews our commitment to be part of the leadership of our country. Bravo. Patricia!"

FRANCES WRIGHT, Founder, *Famous 5 Foundation*

## Two Ways to Enrich Your Next Meeting or Conference

1. **Invite Patricia Morgan to speak to your group**:
   Patricia, *The Bounce Back Expert*, will confidently affirm, "You're stronger than you think." Presenting to thousands of people each year, she is an international speaker with a Master's Degree in Psychology. When you get Patricia, you get practical how-to's that decrease stress and miscommunication while increasing resilience, vitality, joy, productivity and workplace satisfaction. Patricia is renown for delivering her message in a fun, insightful and uplifting manner.

2. **Order a copy of this book for everyone in your organization**:
   Support your people in strengthening their resilience, self-awareness, problem-solving ability and productivity.

To book Patricia Morgan for your next event
or to order any of these books in quantity
please call **(403) 242 • 7796**
or online <**www.solutionsforresilience.com**>

## Endorsements of Patricia Morgan

"Patricia gave us a positive and fun spin on being more resilient at work, including leaving some worry behind."

AMY OSHANYK, *ATB Financial MasterCard*

~

"Just being in the same room as Patricia Morgan is a stress reliever."

KAY OLSEN, *Women in Business*

~

"Patricia Morgan offers a delicious combination of relationship insight, brilliant humour, and practical how-to tips with a delivery style that makes you just want to listen and listen."

BRIAN LEE, CSP, President, *Custom Learning Systems*

# About Patricia Morgan

P ATRICIA is an author and expert in strengthening resilience. She has devoted her life to helping others become stronger and face life's adversities. As *The Bounce Back Expert*, she confidently affirms, "You're stronger than you think."

Presenting to thousands of people each year, she is an international speaker with a Master's Degree in Psychology. She has had careers as a Career Transition Counsellor, Early Childhood Educator, College Instructor, Family Counsellor, Therapeutic Counsellor and Group Facilitator.

In 2003 Patricia was honored by *Global TV* and the YWCA as a *Woman of Vision*. Residing in Calgary, Alberta, Canada, she is the mother to three grown children, grandmother to four and happily married…most days.